MW00596144

Where the Wisteria Grows

Where the Wisteria Grows

Renée G. Mullinax

ISBN-13: 978-1499399882
ISBN-10: 149939988X
© 2014 by B. Renée Mullinax. All rights reserved.
No part of this publication may be reproduced, stored in a retrieval system, or transmitted in any way by any means, electronic, photocopy, recording, or otherwise without the prior permission of the author except as provided by USA copyright law.

Acknowledgements

I express my love and appreciation for:
...my immediate and extended family, who have provided
constant support and sustenance throughout this journey;
...my community of faith and vast network of friends and friends of
friends, who have helped hold me steady with their support,
encouragement, prayer, and compassion;

...Amanda, my patient and indulgent editor, who rose lovingly to
the challenge of her Mother's lack of techno skills;

...Carrie Michal and Bethany Cullen, my designers, whose skills and
artistry helped create the end product;

...my advance readers, for their gracious willingness to read this
manuscript.

...Tenya Shook Reed, whose artistic guidance helped to create a
gnarly, old tree made beautiful in a gown of wisteria.

To God be the glory, for great things He has done

FOREWORD

Let me not to the marriage of true minds
Admit impediments. Love is not love
Which alters when it alteration finds,
Or bends with the remover to remove;
O, no! It is an ever-fixéd mark,
That looks on tempests and is never shaken;
It is the star to every wandering bark,
Whose worth's unknown, although his height be
taken.

William Shakespeare
Sonnet 109

Table of Contents

Introduction

family: Fabaceae (pea family)
subfamily: Faboideae
genus: wisteria, named in memory of Dr. Caspar Wistar by botanist Thomas Nuttall
habitat: eastern United States, China, Korea, and Japan
description: vines that climb by twining stems either clockwise or counterclockwise around any available support; produce blooms in white and in various shades of purple/violet.

Wisteria is an obnoxious plant that claims trees, bushes, fences, and hedgerows. It claims plants many people claim are more obnoxious than wisteria itself. Its roots and arms wrap around anything within its grasp, like a brown and green boa, thick and strangling. It seeks to shroud itself in tiny green leaves during the summer, but we who know it also know that nothing short of digging up its deepest root or bulldozing our property can rid us of it. Indeed, only kudzu gives it adequate competition.

Wisteria is extremely hardy and fast growing, thriving in full sun, growing in fairly poor-quality soils. Mature wisteria can become immensely strong, with heavy, wrist-thick trunks and stems.

Yet for a few short weeks in the southern spring it graces our towns and countryside with the most beautiful, gentle flowers that dangle so delicately from tender green hands. In white and in shades of violet, it exudes a sweet, pleasant aroma that permeates the warm days and cool evenings. Indeed, its smell is so subtle yet so seductive that we briefly forget the power of the plant that produces it. In fact, I suspect that many of us Southerners find ourselves forgiving wisteria of its sins, as long as it will bloom near us.

So much in life is like wisteria. The voracious, twisting, unstoppable events in life can easily choke and destroy, taking over the most finely cultivated field and the most manicured garden.

Yet some of us plant it, for if you dig up a root and put it in the yard, you can have a beautiful bush that will give you sweet flowers if you keep the growth of the bush under control. You have to prune and keep the roots from spreading, for they will surely take charge and wind their destructive tentacles around anything in their path. Wisteria blossoms quickly wither and fall to the ground, exposing the twisted roots and vines that bear them.

But the blossoms in our lives do not drop off. They may get a little tired and faded-looking at times, but they cling, knowing somehow that flowers and root go together to make a whole plant.

For Gary…. and for the glory of God

1
EdVenture

I went to Columbia the day after Christmas to help Amanda, our oldest daughter, with the children. Amanda was sick, so I did what any normal, loving mother and grandmother does when the need arises. Samuel was five, with long blond hair that fell around his fair beautiful face like a punk rocker. He is dangerously precocious, loves maps, and had already found Madagascar on a magnetic map I gave him for his fifth birthday. Hannah was three, with platinum-colored long curls that danced around her pink-cheeked cherubic face that said, "I've got personality!" To give Amanda some peace and quiet (which you don't get with two little people unless they are asleep), I took the children to Ed Venture.

You have to experience this interactive playhouse to appreciate its innovative approach to education. Here kids can climb into a real fire truck, slide down the pole, visit a "farm" and "milk" a life-size cow that moos. They can gather eggs, watch videos of the pasteurization process, crawl in and out and on top of an "igloo," play ice hockey on fabricated ice, do the luge, and otherwise wander from one exhibit to another throughout this huge complex that offers a wide range of hands-on opportunities to get a taste and view of vocations, lifestyles, and possibilities that await the growing mind.

Remember, this was the week of Christmas. The place was full of children of all ages full of excitement and wonder, compounding the energy and excitement of Christmas and not having to be in school.

I was a wad of anxiety, realizing quickly that both my charges needed at least one pair of eyes per child. They were well-behaved;

Amanda had preached, "Stay with Mimi," and "Do as she tells you" with an evangelical zeal. But my eyes were never still, constantly moving from Samuel to Hannah, feeling near panic if I lost sight of them for five seconds.

Of course, that's because, in a crowded place full of highly-charged little people, getting lost or separated is a very real possibility. But there was far more to my anxiety than that. I was thinking about predators. How many were wandering around in the roiling sea of wired children, just looking for a fair-haired, innocent, unsuspecting victim? When it was time to leave so Hannah could have her afternoon nap, I couldn't have made our exit quicker if lava had been behind us.

That got me to thinking: did my parents have such fear or anxiety back in the idyllic 50s when we were on Daytona Beach on July 4 with tens of thousands of other people lying toe-to-toe on the sand while several lanes of cars crept up and down the beach, or when Daddy took us to the boardwalk at night to ride the roller coaster, tilt-a-whirl, bumper cars, and carousel? Or when he took us to the Christmas parade down Main Street on cold winter days?

I don't think so. Oh, they knew there were bad people lurking about, and they exercised reasonable, sensible caution, teaching us to be wary of strangers and to stay within sight and to be obedient.

On the mill village where I was born and grew up, we baby boomers played until well after dark on warm summer nights, chasing each other across dark backyards in games of hide-and-go-seek or cowboys, Indians and outlaws. In winters when we had snow, we stayed outside, sledding down the steep driveway between our house and the Bowens', even after dark.

We were not afraid. We left bikes in the yard, keys in the car, clothes on the line, and didn't even have a key to the house. In the summer, we slept with the windows open. The heat of a southern summer night filled the house, as did the sound of crickets,

Where the Wisteria Grows

the smell of honeysuckle from the "pasture" between the row of houses on Spring Street and the railroad track behind, and the annoying, bombastic horn of the locomotive and the screech of its wheels as it lumbered toward the cotton warehouse half a mile away.

I hated that train. I declared the engineer fell asleep on that horn. You couldn't talk on the one rotary-dial phone that we had without interference from the blast of that horn. It was worse in the summertime with the house open.

In the summer you could know what the neighbors had for supper: fried chicken, fried pork chops, cabbage, beans of some kind, cornbread, coffee. If there was a television in the house, you could know what they were watching: *Andy Griffith*, *Bonanza*, *Dick Van Dyke*, *Gunsmoke*, *I Love Lucy*, and on Saturday mornings, *Lassie*, *Fury*, *The Roy Rogers Show*. Every afternoon of school days, *The Mickey Mouse Club* with Annette and Bobby were a necessary part of life after school was out. And there was always Walter Cronkite, Chet and David. If the neighbors had an argument or a fight during the summer, you knew that, too. But that was rare. I'm sure some of them fought, but we didn't know it.

We were not afraid. We went to the village school, grades 1-7, after which we went to Parker High, for many years one of the best schools in the Southeast; we attended a village church, either Baptist, Methodist, Assembly of God, or Church of God. I never knew a Catholic until high school, and I never knew a Jewish person until I married and moved to New Orleans. People could shop at the company store where Mr. Emerson was the butcher and where there was a soda fountain, a barber shop, and, upstairs, a dry goods department. There was a gym, ball field, and laundromat on the village. On Thursdays Mother went regularly to the Kash and Carry, a very large locally owned supermarket. I loved to go with her and walk – by myself – down the aisles of coffee and the aisles of laundry detergent.

Daddy loved crowds; that's why we went to Daytona the week

Where the Wisteria Grows

of July 4, the only week off the mill workers got. That's why he took us to the parade. That's why he loved to do his shopping on Christmas Eve. He always wanted his family to be with him, although Mother didn't care for the parade or Christmas Eve shopping, so she stayed home and cooked. Daddy kept his eye on us and reminded us to keep our eyes on him, but we were not afraid.

I grew up in the 50s and 60s – a bona fide baby boomer, living in a calm safe world filled with love, security, and encouragement, where the adults in my life who were denied so much education and opportunity worked hard long days so their children could have better than they had had.

So I thought about these things that day at EdVenture, looking for predators. Like I'd know one if I saw one. I remember when I read *The Godfather*. For a long time I looked askance not just at strangers but even people I knew, wondering if he or she was one of those people. Quiet criminals. Part of families who lived dark and dangerous lives in dark and dangerous worlds.

In a small community 20 miles east of the mill village, Gary Mullinax was growing up with his three sisters, a father who was a millwright, and a mother who stayed home, cooked, and took care of children – things mothers did when I was growing up.

2
Once Upon a Life

Most of the mothers I knew who worked outside the home worked in the mill. A few worked other places, like Mildred across the street who worked for a nearby hardware company, and Blanche, who lived on the corner and had her own beauty shop where she and her sister still did fingerwaving styles in the 60s.

My mother had been a traveling saleslady for Freidman's Jewelers. This was during the early 50s, before my sister Rita Kay was born. Mother's territory was the mountains of Greenville, Pickens, and Oconee Counties. Because she was beautiful, charming, and delightful, she sold jewelry effortlessly and so successfully my parents were able to buy the only new car they ever had. Many of her customers were bootleggers who paid for their merchandise from wads of cash in their wallets or the pockets of their overalls. However, the company discontinued their traveling sales program, so Mother was without a job, which was just as well, since my sister would soon be making her appearance in the world, and I would be going to school. The cold winter days when my brother and I would sit at my little formica-top table and eat cornbread and pinto bean soup, our favorite dinner, in the small, mill house kitchen warm with Mother's love and the residual heat from the oven where she had baked the cornbread – those days would be replaced by a schoolroom with wooden floors in a three-story brick schoolhouse across from the mill.

The long, towering, three-story textile mill was the creation of the Woodside brothers: John T., J. David, and Edward. They formed the Woodside Cotton Mill Company in 1902. Raw cotton was delivered by rail to the mill where the complete milling process would take place. The mill not only commanded the premier presence; it provided jobs, steady work, housing, schools, churches, recreation, stores, and an odd sense of family. My father quit school when he was 14 years old and went to work in the mill. That was common. Times were hard. My father liked school, and one of his teachers came to his house to plead for "Johnny to stay in school." He went to the mill, as his brother and sister did later. He became an accomplished loom mechanic, working long, hard hours. When we children came along, he never turned down an opportunity to work overtime.

He always showered and changed clothes before coming home. He didn't want to "smell like the mill and wear lint home." So the mill had its part in educating, feeding, and clothing us. My brother played termite league and little league baseball in the ball field at the end of our street. We played basketball at the fine gym behind the school two blocks away. Once, there had even been a swimming pool where the playground was when we were growing up. Oddly, cotton, which provided our livelihoods and community, was something I had seen only in the huge bales stacked behind the mill or loaded on the freight car. I was 12 years old when I saw a field of cotton on the outskirts of Greenville. I did not know that, about that time, Gary Mullinax was helping his father pick cotton on the few acres they owned, a mile outside of nearby Greer.

When I went to the eighth grade, I went to Parker High School. The campus was very large – so large, in fact, that we had 15 minutes to change class, and if your class was on the other side of the campus from where you were, you needed every second of those fifteen minutes. However, eighth-graders didn't change class. We remained in a self-contained classroom except for music and, I think, some physical ed. We were housed on the third floor of what was referred to as "the eighth-grade building" – a brick edifice almost as large as the elementary school where I'd spent the last seven years. I don't remember how many eighth-grade classrooms there were, but I do remember feeling so overwhelmed and dwarfed by the juniors and seniors whose classes filled the rest of the building. I was always the smallest in my class, except maybe for Pansy Reeves. When it was time to go to the restroom, I became the Queen of Anxiety, fearing a senior might be in there. Going into that huge cafeteria killed my appetite for the first half of the year, even though we eighth graders stayed together – protected from the looming, threatening shadows of upperclassmen. The school was so large there were three lunch periods. There were so many of these big people that the only sanctuary for us low-lifes was my classroom and Miss Margaret Bennett.

Ninth graders changed classes – a concept I did not understand, so I went from being an eighth-grade wreck to a ninth-grade wreck. I had to move around that huge campus from first to second to third period, to lunch, up and down stairs, surrounded by a moving sea of young adults who seemed to know exactly what they were doing, where they were going, and oblivious to the Queen of Anxiety.

By the time I was a sophomore, I was not completely in the game, but at least I was in the dugout. A new junior high school had been built two miles away to house sixth, seventh, and eighth grades. My brother was in the first class there. He didn't have to suffer being swallowed by the aliens in the eighth-grade building.

Of course, that wouldn't have happened to him. He was handsome, rich in leadership skills, congenial, and wanted to do stuff, like play ball, be class president, and sing (which he was very good at, even having the lead in *"Li'l Abner"* when he was a junior at Parker). And he never had an ego problem.

Well, I wanted to do stuff, too, and somewhere inside of me

I knew I had the ability, but I was afraid to step out. I wanted to be with the crowd that wore cranberry and pink, Bass Weejuns, carried John Romaine purses and wallets, be the soloist in our renowned school chorus, chosen for the best parts by the beautiful Esther Rogers (she was former Miss South Carolina and wore Estee Lauder Youth Dew perfume). I was afraid of failing, so I dreamed.

I come from a long line of musically gifted people, on both sides of the family. I was sitting at the piano playing the "Boogie Woogie" long before my feet could touch the floor. I could always hear and sing melodies and harmonies. My brother has always been the same way. I would go home from school and play the pieces we were working on in Mrs. Rogers' class. Once the girls' chorus sang at a meeting of the Greenville Garden Club in an old historic home near the city library, and I did accompany with my accordion. There she was again: Queen of Anxiety. But I did it for a rendition of "Down in the Valley." I was so proud of myself you would think I would have captured some confidence. However, it would be a few years before that would happen.

That would be after I met Gary Mullinax.

3
Hair

Until the Beatles brought their brand of revolution to us, men wore their hair in G.I., "flat-top," crew-cut styles, or cut real short and usually parted on the right or left. The flat-tops were plastered with Butch Hair Wax so that the front would stand straight up, no matter what the weather. My father had real black hair when he was younger, and he parted it on the left and soaked it with some hair tonic or Brylcreem so it would stay put. How could it go anywhere when it was greased to the scalp? My brother had a neat flat-top that was kept in shape by hair wax and the barber at the shop down by the company store.

Those were the days of "flips," French twists, chignons, beehive do's, lacquer, sleeping with hair wrapped with brush rollers or bathroom tissue rolls covered in Kleenex tissue, and bleached hair, since the road to being sexy was paved with blondes whose hair was not only immovable but also indestructible, even in the back seat of a car.

Hair was important. I had a classmate, an only child shamelessly indulged, who got her hair done in a beauty shop twice a week! Her parents were not rich by any stretch, but you would think so to look at her. (She also went regularly to Merle Norman studio.)

So one of the first things I noticed about Gary Mullinax the first time I saw him in the cafeteria at Charleston Southern University was his hair – thick, rich, chestnut-colored, and perfectly parted on the left and groomed.

It was longer than that of most of the other guys. It looked as if it had been brushed, not combed, and there was not a trace of hair grease of any kind. His hair looked free and healthy and practically glistened. I wanted to touch it, but doing so might blemish it in some way.

Not that I would have touched it. I didn't even know his name – yet. I'd have to get that information first.

The other first thing I noticed was how thin and tall he was. You might be tempted to think all of that rich hair would make him topple over. He must have sensed someone was staring at him.

Well, someone was, and when he turned and smiled – a beautiful, warm, honest smile – I was enchanted. It would take a while before I realized the spell would last a lifetime.

Where the Wisteria Grows

4
Different Notes

When I was 12, I began learning to play the guitar. I had always wanted to, mainly because I had seen cowboys play guitars, and anything a cowboy did, especially riding horses, I wanted to do. My grandmother Amanda knew a few chords and songs. Our neighbor Blanche did, too, and she actually had a guitar in the attic. I badgered her until she brought it down. With further pestering, she taught me how to tune it (by ear) and taught me some chords. Seems as if the rest was easy. Grandmother would play for me and teach me too, for I managed to talk Blanche into loaning me the old brown box she had. I pestered Daddy until he bought me a fourstring plastic guitar from the nearby hardware store. This guitar had a picture of Elvis and a hound dog painted on the front, and it had a plastic box that snapped onto the neck. The box had buttons that would make chords – I guess a little like an autoharp. I would lift the box and see which strings were being pressed on which frets. Thus, I learned more chords. I never had to learn which ones to use next when I wanted to play a song; I just seemed to know. I never learned the names of most of the chords I played, but as time went by, I learned seventh, augmented, minor and their degrees. I didn't know their names. I just used them. When my brother began to play and took some lessons, I learned from him.

About that same time, I was learning to play the accordion. That's another story.

Like I mentioned, my family was musical. On hot summer nights Mother would sit on the porch with us. Barry and I would play, and all of us would sing. Mother would join us, kicking in more harmony in the popular rock n' roll songs. After I turned 14, I was always part of a church choir or school choral group.

So shortly after I met Gary Mullinax – something which happened very shortly after seeing him that day in the cafeteria – the music which had been so very natural and normal all of my life was called into service.

Gary was a ministerial student and was one of the leaders of a short devotional and prayer time several mornings a week, very early. These students led weekend and youth revival services in area churches around Charleston and the Lowcountry.

In the fall of 1967, a church in St. George, S.C., started a mission in a small place with the odd name of Pregnall. Gary was asked to be the pastor. He accepted, and then turned to me. He needed a piano player.

There we began our ministry. I wasn't very good; I had only played by ear, although, along the way, I had learned to read music and also learned conducting patterns.

The church was an old but neat frame building with a few rooms to the side and back of the sanctuary. It was a quaint, picturesque structure a short distance from the highway that runs from Summerville to St. George. It sat about 50 yards off a county road that was paved for a short distance before giving way to a sandbed road, one of many in the Lowcountry in those days. Large moss-covered, gnarled oaks stood between the church and the road. Of course, there was no air conditioning – only funeral home fans swishing through the air on those hot, humid summer Sundays. Gary always wore a suit when he was in the pulpit. This was a time when custom and tradition dictated attire, no matter the weather. And in the deep South, heat, mosquitoes, gnats, and humidity are a constant nine months a year. We worked there through the summer of 1968. We learned much, the people were kind, patient country folks, and love grew.

Where the Wisteria Grows

Then he finished his degree and announced he would be going to seminary in New Orleans. If I had been more mature and less naïve, I would not have been surprised. I had just completed my freshman year. What was I supposed to do? I suggested we get married and go to New Orleans together. Besides, I didn't have enough money to go back to Charleston Southern.

He had already thought through all of this. "You go back home, enroll at North Greenville. I will be back."

That is what we did.

Where the Wisteria Grows

5
Roads

The highway north from Greenville, toward what was then North Greenville Junior College, was once a two-lane, twisting road winding through upper Greenville County, where the most southern bounds of the Blue Ridge Mountains grace the approaching eye. My parents and Uncle Ray and Aunt Dot together owned a small piece of property tucked back in the woods, off a dirt road, and bordered by a clear stream which we crossed over on a wooden bridge. Daddy and Uncle Ray built a rambling one-room cabin, where Mother and Aunt Dot cooked on an old Home Comfort wood stove.

This was in the early 50s, before my sister was born. Barry and I played in the cold water of the creek, while Daddy and Uncle Ray hammered and sawed, continuing to frame the cabin, and Mother and Aunt Dot cooked. In those days, much of the Upstate of South Carolina was still considered the "Dark Corner," especially in the mountains, but we didn't know that, and it would not have mattered much if we had. Besides, times were changing; electricity and running water were rapidly coming to even the most isolated communities, and mobility and exposure to the rest of the world were hurtling toward the coves and deep hollers of the Upstate counties. Schools and compulsory attendance laws were bringing children out of generations of ignorance and grinding poverty and from fields where mule-drawn plows had wrenched potatoes, beans, and corn from rocky soil.

The cabin was still a work in progress when the city of Greenville bought thousands of acres of mountains, streams, and valleys for the city's watershed. We had to sell what Mother called Lazy City.

In 1968, when I drove the one family car, a '63 Buick, to school, U.S. 25 was already a smooth, four-lane highway that provided beautiful views the further north I drove. I never tired of the gentle, quiet, distant mountains that I knew were getting closer with every mile I drove. During that fall my eyes drank the rich yellows, browns, reds, ambers, and oranges, watching them daily as Mother Nature dipped her brush into her palette and deepened her picture, making each days' colors richer than the day before. As the cool of autumn moved steadily toward the cold of winter, I watched the leaves of autumn turn dull and drift to the gray ground below. Sometime in January, not long after Christmas, snow fell, and the ridges and peaks wore white coats and caps that sparkled like crystal in the winter sunlight.

Meanwhile, Gary was in school and had gotten a job at Red Ball Freight Company. I had gotten a job on weekends in the employee cafeteria at Greenville General Hospital.

When he arrived at seminary, he found his tuition had already been paid by our religion professor at Charleston Southern. Gary had been a grader for him. Still, he had to eat and live, so he worked until he was laid off in February. Then he got real hungry and picked up Coke bottles to sell in order to buy TV dinners.

We wrote to each other every day. His letters were well-written. He had minored in English in college and had always loved to read – an important factor in writing well. He enjoyed poetry, philosophy, history. He would read anything. After we were married he once stayed up all night reading Dostoevsky's *The Brothers Karamozov*. More importantly, his letters were warm, loving, romantic, full of honest passion, yet never mushy or trite. Words that would have otherwise been clichés were profound, rich and intense when he wrote them. There was never anything false about him. The letters were beautiful to read, and I anxiously awaited them each day. Some days I got more than one.

Where the Wisteria Grows

Roads between lovers are hard and lonely, no matter how many or few are the miles that separate you or how many others who love you are around. Hearts that are meant to be together beat with an irregular rhythm when separated.

By March he had had enough of being hungry and lonely. He came home to Greer, went to work with his Dad at Daniel Construction, we saved our money, I finished North Greenville in May, and we married in July, 1969, in a simple wedding at my church on the mill village, right across from the mill. Mother's sister, Aunt Curt, made the cake, and she and Aunt Versa Lee, the oldest sister, made my dress. Cousin Jamelle did my hair, Barry sang "True Love," Aunt Dot and Nora Elledge decorated with magnolias, and a friend from North Greenville played the organ, including "A Time for Us," from Romeo and Juliet. The reception in the church fellowship hall consisted of mints, nuts, punch, and cake squares. It would be a few years before I learned wedding receptions could be catered and serve elaborate dishes I had mostly never heard of, and, furthermore, would provide full bars – alcohol, for heaven's sakes! By the time our older children married in the 90s, one reception was catered at a nearby plantation, and our son's rehearsal party was at our house where I hosted an oyster roast and pig-pickin'.

I had come a long way from my mill village church wedding. And still no alcohol. But I was just as married, even without champagne, cucumber sandwiches, a string quartet, and a dance floor. I never could dance, anyway. I didn't realize I had planted my first wisteria bush.

Now, 45 years after that July night when two virgins came together in a Holiday Inn honeymoon suite just outside of Hendersonville, N.C., I am more married than ever, for the song of my own heart has never stopped singing to me.

Where the Wisteria Grows

We moved into a single-wide mobile home on the seminary campus. Gary had already paid several months' rent. In less than a month, Hurricane Camille made its way toward us. I begged Gary to move inland, but we rode out the storm with friends who lived in an upstairs apartment on campus. I stayed up all night, watching the massive old trees that graced the campus bend almost to the ground (miraculously, they survived). Every now and then a massive ball of fire would light the sky as a transformer blew. I remember thinking of Margaret Mitchell's description of the shelling of Atlanta and the raging fires as Scarlett, Rhett, Prissy, Melanie, and a newborn fled the conflagration in a rickety wagon pulled by an old spavin horse Rhett had stolen.

Gary slept that night. As we were soon to learn, the fury of the storm landed just east, along the Mississippi coast, destroying the antebellum homes that had stood the ravages of man and Mother Nature for generations. In less than two years, Gary and I would go to Pass Christian to pastor the little Baptist church just two blocks from the beach. It had suffered only a small broken window to testify to the fickle nature of one of the most powerful forces our planet devises.

We had wonderful neighbors around us at seminary. Harry and Sharon Warren were newlyweds, too, and we began a friendship that has remained steadfast and sure. Harry and Gary were avid hunters and fishermen. During the school year, they taught school in the afternoons in the very crowded district in Westwego, across the Mississippi River. It was a convenient arrangement, as they could attend their own classes in the mornings. Sharon and I got good jobs downtown at Mobil Oil.

I didn't really have any job skills other than operating a switchboard, so that is what I did. During the summer when school was out, Harry and Gary went fishing. They had bought a piece of a boat that they repaired and fiber-glassed and named Nimrod, a biblical character who was known as a great fisherman. They spent so much time together in that old boat I threatened to move in with Sharon and just send Harry to stay at our place.

Where the Wisteria Grows

Sharon and I had to get up early every morning to go to our jobs while our husbands were leaving for the lakes, canals, and brackish creeks that almost define Orleans Parish.

I enjoyed New Orleans, although I didn't get away from a train. Instead, I got closer. About a half dozen tracks were just beyond the seminary fence, and trains were constantly moving. It seemed as if they ran straight through our small bedroom. Sometimes trains would pass each other and our entire trailer would tremble as if in an earthquake.

Those of us who didn't have children usually fared better at seminary. Many of the students had left other vocations and uprooted their families from all they had known to follow what they believed was God's purpose for their lives. They came from the Carolinas, Georgia, Florida, Alabama, Kentucky, Mississippi, Arkansas, Virginia – from communities and cousins who mostly believed as they did, mostly obeyed the rules, and sang Southern gospel. The Bible was inerrant, souls were for saving, fried chicken was the belt around the Baptist preacher's waist, and lard was the right thing in which to fry the chicken. Children were to do as told and be respectful, and Catholics, while good folks, were mostly suspect and needed to be saved. Episcopalians and Lutherans were passable, but Jews were God's chosen.

So these families moved to New Orleans, and, for many, it was nothing short of culture shock. One trip to Bourbon Street could, at best, soil your soul and assure you of a Pilate complex, or, at worst, doom you with its seduction.

Wives had to find work so husbands could go to school. Children had to enroll in city schools, and couples struggled to pay bills and adjust. Seminary campus, where most students lived, provided an insular community of faith and shared values – a haven from the strange world outside the campus gates, where restaurants served whole boiled crabs and shrimp, served beer by the pitcher, and where patrons were often loud and raucous and had no inhibitions about enjoying themselves.

Our life, however, was mostly free from encumbrances. We had time to learn each other. I made friends and met wonderful people, both on campus and out in the city. Many of the students took part-time pastorates of small churches in Louisiana, Mississippi, and even Alabama. Harry took a small church not far from Columbia, Mississippi. On weekends these men loaded their families and traveled to the church field. Gary did some of this work on an interim and substitute basis until the church in Pass Christian called us.

That was in 1971. We moved to the church field that summer, after filling in for a few months. Like the church, the parsonage survived Camille, but most of that small town was in ruins. Gary commuted to seminary for a while, but after three quarters, he decided he had the tools he needed. He left, never went back, and never regretted his decision.

Where the Wisteria Grows

6
Big Easy

Mardi Gras is a grand, free party with no walls, wide-open admission, and few rules. Don't shoot anybody, gang up on anybody, or try to steal a drink. Put on a costume, go to the parades that occur nightly prior to Fat Tuesday, spend that day in The Quarter, and, if you want to spend money, you most certainly can. The narrow streets can offer the most elaborate, extreme, inventive, and lively sideshow in the country. In this atmosphere, drunkenness and drug-induced highs can be a birthright, or at least a celebratory right. Extreme mental disorders might be just part of the party.

I enjoyed the parades and the energy of this party. We happened to be there the year the festival celebrated its centennial. My friend Marie and I went to parades (Gary didn't care for the crowds), and we leapt with upstretched arms to catch the doubloons, costume jewelry, and other bubble-gum-machine trinkets, many of which were commemorative of the centennial. I kept them for a long time and would take them to school during Lent and talk about them, tying them into the meaning of Carnival – information so foreign to my Lowcountry Protestant children. I haven't seen that bag of souvenirs in years. I don't know if they were lost during one of our moves, or if I hid them too well.

I didn't wear a costume, but I sure enjoyed the ones others wore. I saw a man dressed as a caveman, a family of five all dressed as the Statue of Liberty, and a flower child wearing nothing but an artificial bunch of grapes around his waist, a fake fruit crown on his long hair, carrying a basket of real fruit, and walking barefoot on the streets and sidewalks that reeked of stale beer and urine. When he walked, the bunch of grapes in front and back would sway.

Gary did go with me on the actual day. We enjoyed the occasion, and, two years later when we were living in Pass Christian, one of our church members, whose husband was a retired cardiologist and a bona fide Cajun, gave us tickets to the Rex Comus ball. I was ghastly sick in the early months of pregnancy with Amanda, but I would have gone to that ball if I had had to hire an ambulance. I guess I knew I would never again see so much mink, ermine, and so many jewels. Looking back into that memory, I would say being there was next to being in the presence of the Queen of England or at the Oscars.

If I had known what we were to face in years to come, I would have known that those early years, the 70s and 80s when there was so much work, the children were growing, our ministry was active and vibrant – I would have understood that, in a very odd sense, our lives then were a kind of festival – a festival of productive, healthy days, many of which were normally frustrating and challenging yet constantly, consistently blessed with God's grace and attendance, his presence felt by and through the lives he put in ours so we could be encouraged, sustained, and so loved.

Where the Wisteria Grows

7
Shangpo & Ehrhardt

I have never been to China. Our youngest daughter went with a school group a few years ago. I read Pearl Buck's books and short stories, and I like most Chinese food. I am a fan of Chinese martial arts, but I can't do any. Most of what I know about China is its growing power on the world stage. It remains strongly Communist, but good ole' Western capitalism has become an increasingly strong force. It seems to be a country whose britches can't keep up with its growth – like an awkward adolescent. Its cities are sprawling, teeming centers of impressive buildings, superb technology, and thriving business hubs, all indicators of wealth and economic health. It is easy and tempting to think that all is well and comfortable in China.

Twelve hundred miles from Beijing is the small village of Shangpo. To go there is to step through the scrim of time, for it is a place where farmers work barefooted in the rice fields, and life appears unchanged – a place where people live their daily days as they have for generations.

Like most people everywhere, Shangpo villagers just want to live their lives, feed their families, go about their days with reasonable contentment, peace, and security. Just get along in life.

However, it isn't that simple. Ambitious, dangerous people who want power have threatened these villagers and conspired with a local leader to take their property. They have come in cars and are armed with very modern, effective weapons. To the intruders' surprise, the villagers have fought back, demanding democratic

Where the Wisteria Grows

reforms and justice – a mini-revolt in a tiny place far away from the skyscrapers and Wi-fi of the rest of the world.

There are similar places all over the world, small villages and towns that time seems to have forgotten, where families' ancestors settled hundreds of years ago. The people all know each other and are often related. Most of them mind their own business when not minding their neighbors'.

In 1972, we moved to one of these communities. The Baptist Church in Ehrhardt, S.C., called Gary to be their pastor. The church flew Gary to Savannah, where a friend met him and took him to Ehrhardt to meet with the pastor search committee. I was very pregnant with Amanda, so I stayed in Pass Christian that weekend. That was probably a good thing. With my impulsive personality and tendency to shoot from the hip, the outcome may have been quite different.

When Gary returned, I asked, "Is the church in the country?"

"The whole town is in the country!" he replied.

Within two weeks, on a hot August day, we moved. The church flew me to Augusta where two ladies from the church met me. Of course, they and I did not know what each other looked like. Gary had just told them, "She's got brown hair, and she's very pregnant." As it turned out, I was the only woman on the plane, so they found me easily.

Meanwhile, Gary was driving a U-Haul, accompanied by our Irish setter, and pulling our Ford Pinto station wagon. (That's what we called them before the days of SUVs and mini-vans designed to haul car seats, children, and dogs.)

The ride from Augusta to Ehrhardt took about an hour and a half. The countryside became more isolated, flat and swampy. I went through towns I had never heard of: Williston, Denmark, Bamberg. Ms. Llewelyn pointed out the courthouse in Bamberg, an imposing, old brick building on the north side of the railroad tracks that divided the town. "That's our county seat," she said. Then she

Where the Wisteria Grows

turned right and drove down U.S. 601 toward Ehrhardt. Once we left the Bamberg town limits, there was little else. We crossed the Salkehatchie River and Lemon Swamp, where the black water quietly and almost imperceptibly moves around the gnarled cypress knees. The trees wore long beards of Spanish moss. Occasionally there would be a field of soybeans or drying corn here and there, crops waiting for harvest within the next two months.

Fifteen minutes after we left Bamberg we entered the town limits of Ehrhardt. The distance between one town limit sign and the other was one mile. There was very little there. The main street consisted of Herndon's large livestock market, a small furniture store, Copeland's General Store, Farmer's Trade Store, The Grapevine (a small clothing store for women), Waggoner's Feed and Seed, Ehrhardt Grocery (owned and operated by Claude Hiers, who still made home deliveries), a post office, a bank, three service stations, and a liquor store behind the Farmer's Trade Store. The church was a block off the main street, Highway 601, which, if you traveled south 15 more miles, would take you to Hampton, S.C.

Ms. Llewellyn and Mary Jo showed me the parsonage, and I could not believe I would be living in such a large, fine home. The church was a neat brick building across the quiet street.

That day I had come to the town that would be my home for the next 32 years. Our four children would be born and would grow up in a place where we did not lock our doors, where they could ride their bikes anywhere, I could keep the horse I would soon get in the pasture behind Herndon's and ride down the sandy roads and around the fields just outside the town, and become so much a part of this small community that stood in a place in time that wasn't the place where time was.

Where the Wisteria Grows

8
People are People are People

Of course, no armed, dangerous men rode into Ehrhardt to take anyone's property. That is not to say there were no armed, dangerous men (or women) there. There was the man who found his wife and her lover together, blew them away with his shotgun (as he had promised her), took the gun to the sheriff's office and told him where the bodies were. He served a rather brief sentence, considering the crime, and was allowed to go back to the farm to harvest his crop.

There was the man who walked into a local store, pulled out a gun, and shot and killed the owner of the store while his young son watched.

There was the local merchant who would loan money during the Depression and charge 100% interest.

There was the woman down the street from the church who gut-shot her husband as he was trying to enter the bedroom window. He failed to identify himself.

Any place where people are is a place where every vice known to humankind exists. Children are molested, abused, neglected; spouses, girlfriends, old people are victimized and brutalized by others sick with their own insecurities, fears, and pasts. Gary used to say, "Ehrhardt is a microcosm of the whole world."

These folks, however, were, thankfully, in the minority. Most people worked, tried to do right, took care of their families, voted during elections, paid their bills, kept a word promised, and usually went to church. The community was quite open. That is to say that our houses were glass where we could see out, others could see in, everybody knew and was probably kin to everyone else. How could it be otherwise when the population was less than 500?

But, as Lavinia Bishop told me when we first came to town, "They will talk about you, criticize you, but when you need help or meet trouble, they will all be there to help you."

She was so right. Time after time, I saw the whole community reach out to its neighbors. No matter how good, bad, or ugly that person may have been, help was not just on the way; it was already there. The time was coming when I would know myself just how big and loving my family of Lowcountry brothers and sisters had become. Too soon they would surround me and hold me through long dark nights and deep valleys, and, with their distinct drawls, pray for me. I would come to recognize, in my neighbors' eyes, hearts that said, "We love you. We are here. We share your loss, grief, pain, joy, and we want to help keep hope alive for all of us."

Where the Wisteria Grows

9
Parenthood & School Days

Amanda Elana: born October 7, 1972
Garren Barrett: born February 5, 1975
Gordon Seth: born April 12, 1980
Carrie Michal: born September 21, 1989

I suppose that's quite a production record for a foolish young woman who had said she didn't want any children. I never felt prepared for motherhood. That didn't change much over the years, either. Then again, how many people are prepared for parenthood? No matter what we read or see, most of our preparation comes in the form of the parents who created us. We tend to parent as we tend to do many things in our lives: we do as we saw things done.

That is another important reason to be grateful Gary and I grew up not only seeing but also knowing love, security, faith, and trust. There were rules, manners, parameters of propriety, honesty, and obedience to those in whose care you have been entrusted.

So those are things we taught. I don't think people necessarily do them consciously. Certain things are, like language, embedded in us. Unfortunately, that can be true of bad things.

Life was never easy. We always seemed to struggle, but we worked and made our way. Thanks to Gary, I had gone back to school, completed my undergraduate work, and taught school the rest of my life.

That is a thing I probably would not have done. He believed in me more than I believed in me. "You like school. I'll help with the children [at the time just Amanda and Garren]. Besides, you never know when you'll really need that degree."

So on a typically hot August day in 1976, he sat outside the Carolina Coliseum in Columbia with the children while I went inside and stood in the long lines to register for that fall semester.

Fortunately, most of my credits transferred into the university. I enrolled as a junior majoring in English education. And Gary was right: I did like school. I took 12 hours, two days a week, three courses back-to-back, beginning at 8 a.m. I had to leave at 6 a.m. to make the long drive to Columbia and arrive on time. The winter of '77 was one of the coldest ever – a time when Lemon Swamp froze, forming black-water icicles on the drooping gray moss and the tops of cypress knees. One January morning as I walked toward the humanities building, a guy was ice skating on the reflection pond. Ice skating!

And Gary was true to his word. He took care of the children. If he needed to go to the hospital to visit, or if other needs arose that required his attention as a pastor, he made sure the children were taken care of. Now I never knew exactly who might have them. There was no daycare center. Often that someone would be my dear friend Carolyn, who rarely said no to me even when she probably should have, or kind Mary Jo, who also rarely said no, or Yvonne, or Aunt Sally. The important thing was they would be in the hands of someone who loved them and would protect them as if my children were theirs. In many ways, they were.

I learned about and read H.L Mencken from Dr. Nolte, a Mencken scholar. I learned literary analysis from the sharp, incisive lectures of Dr. Joel Myerson, who smoked cigarettes while he read from his extensive, provocative lecture notes, and I was fascinated by the origins of the English language, taught by the masterful Dr. Ericka Lindemann, one of the best teachers I had. I did well, finishing by way of correspondence, regional campuses, and closed-circuit TV.

I graduated in '79, took a job at Denmark-Olar High School, a challenging job, and promptly got pregnant with Seth.

Sometimes babies can be so timely. I left the school after the first semester and waited for Baby Seth, our third treasure from God. Another beautiful bloom.

10
Strains of Music & Ministry

I let two friends talk me into teaching piano and guitar – two things I knew I had no business doing. I'd had only six months of "formal" music, but I heard, "Teach what you know." I guess that goes to prove how desperate folks were for someone to teach music to their children, most of whom were very good students for about six months. Brings to mind Condoleezza Rice's answer to the question, "Why didn't you teach music?" "I didn't want to spend my life hearing children butcher Beethoven."

Of course, I couldn't even play Beethoven. So there wasn't much chance of teaching children to mutilate it; I could do it myself. I could read music, but I had no training in theory or technique. I did, however, work at it. I spent far more time practicing, I'm sure, than any child who sat on my piano bench.

I wanted to stay home with Baby Seth, so my friend Ann went with me to the nearest music store (40 miles away) and helped me get beginner music books, and I did my best.

I quickly had a dozen or so piano students and one guitar guy.

Meanwhile, the work of our ministry continued. Gary was quickly becoming everyone's pastor, as the Lutheran and Methodist ministers came and went. Because he knew how to listen with a pastor's heart, and because he never betrayed a confidence (not even to me, when I was dying to know), he gained trust and became everyone's confidante.

He married the young (and sometimes the old), buried the dead, counseled the burdened, spoke eloquently and intelligently from the pulpit, and always made time for whoever stopped him and said, "Preacher, I need to talk with you." He listened without judgment and advised, when asked, with uncanny wisdom. Our neighbor Lavern used to say, "I think Gary was born wise." He baptized the newly converted and led them through a course teaching basic Christian ethics, setting them on a path toward spiritual maturity. If they never made it very far as they moved on, it wasn't his fault. He lived what he taught, and had a tremendous capacity for understanding and tolerance, but everyone knew where he stood.

I often felt like a widow. At daylight, he was sitting in a deer stand. Late afternoon, same thing, if he wasn't called out to the hospital or elsewhere. During duck season, he hunted ducks. Any time was time to go fishing. Summer was for flounder or frog gigging and shrimping. Winter was for gathering oysters off the Lowcountry coast – Beaufort or Edisto Island. In January or February, we went to Searson's, Kinard's, or Priester's and butchered hogs with people whom we would help when their turn came. Neither of us had ever done such a thing, but we learned. We cured our own meat in a box Gary had built and smoked the hams and shoulders in Leon Priester's smokehouse.

In '81 I took a job teaching at the middle school in Barnwell, S.C. I would stay in that district 25 miles away for the next 28 years, taking our children with me to school. It was a wonderful beginning of a decade of growth, learning, and working, not only in the classroom but in music and teaching ministry. All the while we were making investments in people, without realizing how life-sustaining that would be in the coming years.

Where the Wisteria Grows

11
Ladies & Gentlemen

I like men. I like men who will listen, men who don't seek conquest, men who neither intimidate nor seek to intimidate because they are sure of who they are and have no need to impress.

Of course, I've never been around bad men. My father roared a lot, but he had a tender heart, loved us with his total being and would have died a cruel death before letting harm come to us. We were his life. My uncles on both sides were decent, caring men who worked, loved their families, didn't do things to put them in the hoosegow or give them and their families shame, and showed kind affection and honest emotion. I'm sure there were bad men on the village, but I didn't know them, or, if I did, I didn't *know* them. True, no one talked about "such things" as incest, abuse, molestation, and the seemingly limitless depravities of human nature I have since learned are universal. After all, the mill village, like Ehrhardt, was, in Gary's words, "a microcosm of the world." But I didn't know about such things.

I like women, but, there again, most of the women in my life have been decent, caring people. My mother was a crown jewel, as were her sisters. My cousins and I did not know spiteful, abusive women in our lives. I definitely have known a few, and I certainly know how cruel young girls can be. But thank God, such personalities have not shaped me.

Women can be friends with each other in ways men cannot. Women can hug and kiss each other, cry together, hold hands, tell true secrets, and not see each other for years — even decades, yet not miss a beat. Women can be close without being suspect.

Where the Wisteria Grows

When you grow up surrounded by warmth, affection, trust, and faith, you are, I believe, prepared to deal with the vagaries of human nature to which you will eventually be exposed. Badness is not necessarily easy to understand, nor is it meant to be accepted, but it is inherent in our humanity and has its own peculiar immortality. Shakespeare gave the words to Marc Antony in his eulogy for Julius Caesar: "The evil that men do lives after them/but the good is often interred with their bones." I have observed, however, that the real good people do lives after them as well, leaving powerful legacies of generosity, faith, and service to generations who follow them.

Gary was a different kind of man. He possessed all of the attributes the wonderful men in my life had, but he raised the bar with a combination of intelligence, wisdom, gifts of the Spirit, strong leadership skills and sense of fairness, and an astuteness about human behavior that could be downright spooky at times. He was an avid hunter, fisherman, woodworker, and beekeeper. He was a congenial mixer among people yet equally content to sit alone and quietly in a deer stand, in the boat he made and took to the black water of the Salkehatchie, or in our library with a good book in his hands. He had read the works of Nietzsche, Jung, Bonhoeffer, Luther and other great thinkers and theologians. He enjoyed and appreciated opera, theater, and symphony, and was proud of the time he had a bass solo at the Dock Street Theater in Charleston during a choral performance. Because he knew God and knew himself, he was neither afraid of nor intimidated by new or different ideas.

He was never one to fret over things that could not be changed, and he seemed to know instinctively what those immutables were. He was one to move expeditiously on what could be changed. He did not borrow tomorrow's troubles but dealt with the day at hand. He did not believe in going back to places he had once been, so I never went to a Mullinax family reunion or his high school reunion until the class had its 50th.

Where the Wisteria Grows

He had no desire to return to any church we served. He said, "It's never the same. You can't go back and expect all that was once there to still be there. I am a man of the present." A few people took some offense at that, but he never meant it that way. His focus was on now, not then.

He set high expectations for the children, and I am pleased and grateful that we now can say all four of them have played by the rules, never brought us shame, and wear the work ethic and faith their parents had learned and worked to instill in them. So far, so good, as the saying goes.

Our lives were soon to change dramatically and irrevocably, and all of the good things we had during the green years would be required to carry us through the dark years ahead.

12
Family Dinners

When Gary and I were growing up, there were no fast-food franchises. Wouldn't have mattered; our families didn't have any money to go there. I well remember the first McDonald's that opened in Greenville. We had a family friend whom we called Pinky, a bachelor who drove a cab. Every four to six months, he would take a three or four week "leave," so to speak, when he would lie in bed very drunk. Now most of the men in my family drank, but they never missed work, didn't drink all of the time, and certainly didn't lie around drunk. Pinky was a decent, hard-working bachelor who lived with his mother in a shotgun-style house outside the city limits – an area that was in the country then. I never knew of any girlfriends Pinky had, but he adored my mother and my sister Rita Kay. He would have harnessed the moon for Rita. When he went "on leave," my father would take charge of him, for he would literally throw away money if he couldn't give it away fast enough. Daddy would take the money, dole it out carefully, portion out the liquor, and, when Pinky began to sober, give him his money, make him bathe, and generally father him.

The first time I ate at McDonald's was when Pinky was "on leave." He insisted we go to that new hamburger place "over thar on 291." Daddy exclaimed, "Way over thar!" In the late 50s, the "291 bypass" may just as well have been the other side of Atlanta. After all, everyone we knew only had one car. The only car Pinky had was a taxi. "I'll pay for ever'thing, Johnny. Let's take Ruby and th' kids over thar."

So we went. The menu consisted of hamburgers (35 cents), cheeseburgers, fries, milkshakes (three flavors), orange drink, and, I think, Coke. I thought it was wonderful.

Like every other woman I knew, Mother cooked. She and her sisters were fine cooks who took pride in their products. It was important for food to taste good, but it was equally important for it to look good. Mother would garnish potato salad and stuffed eggs with paprika and fresh parsley, and her cakes and pies were works of art. We had large family dinners – often. Mother's birthday was the big occasion, for it was on New Year's Day, children were out of school and parents had the day off. We also got together at Grandpa Cox's for his birthday, or Pete's birthday, or Charles's birthday – didn't matter. Grandpa lived out in the country, and I loved it because there were woods and fields where I could disappear on my imaginary horse. We had gatherings in the small house in the village. If the weather allowed, people would eat outside, standing if there was no place to sit. When my first cousin Joyce and her husband bought a farm outside of Greer, S.C., out in the peach country, they remodeled an old two-story farmhouse, so for years we went there because there was so much room, she and her husband Pete were wonderful hosts, and, best of all, Pete always had fine gaited horses.

Family and food were just regular events, so, as I grew and acquired my own family, it was just natural to have gatherings. For a tomboy who wanted to be Tarzan, Zorro, or the owner of Fury, I became a good cook, especially of the game and fish Gary brought in. Many of the men in my family liked to hunt, and Ehrhardt was a mecca for them. My cousins and I always got along, so the sprawling parsonage in Ehrhardt became the place to be. In the Lowcountry, there are fresh vegetables available most of the year. In the summer, I canned and put food in the freezer. In the fall, and, sometimes during the winter if the weather was mild, there were collards, sweet potatoes, spinach, turnips, lettuces in late spring.

Unlike many women, Mother, my sister, my cousins, and my aunts – we could all work in the kitchen together.

Where the Wisteria Grows

We didn't fuss or complain or criticize. We were too busy having fun, laughing, even singing sometimes, for we all could do that.

It was such a time in October of 1990. We had a big gathering. The hunts had been successful. The weather was warm. We had gone to church together. We never believed in staying home from church to cook. We had a grand time. Amanda was in her first year at the university. Garren was a sophomore in high school. Seth was a very athletic ten-year-old. He would leave home at the age of 15 to train in gymnastics. Carrie Michal was 13 months old.

Gary left shortly after dinner that day. One of his sisters needed him, so he set out for Norfolk, Va. He was to return late the next day.

After the crowd left, I began making preparations for our fall camping trip to the Cataloochee Valley, where the two of us would spend a few days riding horses in that wonderful, beautiful place where the mountains are formed in waves that tower above this special land. All of us went several times a year, but twice a year Gary and I went by ourselves. We all once spent Thanksgiving there, riding the horses from camp to Mt. Sterling and back down via Long Bunk Trail and Little Cataloochee.

On Monday evening as I packed and listened to a Connie Francis tape, there was a knock at the door. Lavern and Leon, our neighbors and deacons, came in. "Gary's been in a bad accident in Virginia," Leon said. "He has suffered a severe head injury." The two men were obviously troubled and trying not to show it.

"Is he alive?" I asked.

"Yes, he's alive," Leon said. "He was taken to the hospital in Emporia but is being transferred to Medical College of Virginia in Richmond." I don't know what it would feel like to be a piece of wood, but, whatever that is, that's where I was.

Leon took the lead. "We gotta git more information."

I learned later that the first word that had come to the sheriff's dispatch in Bamberg was Gary was dead. The sheriff called the mayor of Ehrhardt and relayed that message. The mayor called Leon, who

who was deacon chair at the time.

"Who says Gary is dead? I am not goin' over and tell his wife he's dead if he ain't."

So before he and Lavern came over, Leon had found out that, indeed, Gary was not dead. He was badly hurt, but he was not dead.

By 11 that night, Leon and I were on the road to Richmond. Torrential rain fell all night. I had worked all day Monday, so I lay in the back seat and slept for a short while. We arrived in Richmond at daybreak.

It would be six months before Gary would come home.

13
Richmond

Dawn was just breaking when we arrived at the Medical College of Virginia in Richmond. This was a city I had visited very briefly once when on choir tour my freshman year of college, and again in February of '90 when Gary, Amanda and I went for a commissioning service for Gary's sister Wanda and her husband. They had been appointed to the mission field and would be moving to Kenya. Richmond is a place steeped in history, having been the capital of the Confederacy – a fact I never have understood. Why would the South choose a capital city that is almost in the North?

On this balmy day, the sun peeked through a few wispy clouds left over by the storms of the previous day and night, pushing these small, light-gray puffs aside and aiming its brilliance on a clean, rain-washed world. I did not know what was waiting for me somewhere in that imposing building toward which we walked. Leon led the way, and I followed, glad to have someone with me who could think, who knew the right questions to ask, and who would politely persist until answers were given and understood.

Up and down the streets of that city and nearby neighborhoods, people were getting up, living their daily lives that would take them to work, getting children ready for school, pushing through the hectic fray, going about their everyday routines, making plans – another ordinary day.

Nothing would ever be ordinary again for us. It would take a while for full realization to come to me.

On this morning, we made our way to the 14-bed neurological trauma unit. A nurse led us to a bed on the far side of the unit by a wall. Behind a curtain lay my husband, swollen, attached to more machines than I could count and whose purposes I did not understand except that they must be keeping Gary alive. Leon burst into tears, sobbing, burying his face in his hands, his shoulders heaving. He had recently lost his father, and Gary was like a brother to him. I went to him and put my hand on a trembling shoulder, but I said nothing. I did not cry. I looked down at this 44-year-old man who was my best friend, my confidante, my source of strength and encouragement, my lover, the father of my children, the beloved pastor and mentor to so many, the hunter, fisherman, beekeeper, community leader, and I said and did nothing. What was there to say? What was there to do?

So I stood quietly, feeling no fear, and maybe not feeling much of anything. He was alive. I was alive.

In time, the pain, grief and loss would come in invading waves, never going away completely or for very long. I would soon be learning many lessons; I would have to learn them, for they would become tools for survival.

Leon cried himself out and then apologized. "I'm sorry," he choked, "but I looked at him, and I could see Daddy, and...I just couldn't stop myself."

"Do not apologize any more. It isn't necessary."

I guess at the moment we both were wondering what to do next. That's a funny thing about folks: we think we have to do something.

Well, sometimes we do have to do. Sometimes we don't. Sometimes we don't because we don't know what to do. On this morning, we did not know.

Where the Wisteria Grows

14
Finding Routine

There were things, however, that were quietly yet firmly in control, and they were exercising their power, undetected by the monitors, x-rays, scans, MRIs and white-coated sentinels.

One: Gary's age and good health. He was strong, lean, and had been quite athletic as a young man. He was moderate in his daily habits and never had been one to complain about or give in to the vicissitudes of life.

Two: the vast army of family and friends, including family and friends of family and friends – many people we didn't know – who were praying for him, calling me with encouragement, giving money to a fund set up in his name in our local bank, helping my parents as they now were more parents again than grandparents, and assuring me that "Gary will come back to us," although they may not have been so sure of that themselves. Perhaps a friend of ours at the time who probably knew Gary better than anyone beside me put it this way: "He has too much to come back to, and he knows that."

Three: Gary's own spirit of determination and, at times, downright bull-headedness that had always refused defeat. This somewhat dubious virtue had more than once been a vexation for me, but now, somewhere deep inside of him, it was very alive and on his side, fighting.

Four: A faith that would not let either of us go. The strength and confidence he had spent years infusing in me now rose within me and began to transmit in some inexplicable way between us, empowering us with the conviction that God, who had begun a good work in us, would be faithful to complete it.

So the days slipped into weeks.

Strange how quickly we establish routine. I soon had a daily plan: around 9 a.m. walk the two blocks from the Hospitality House to the hospital and climb the stairs to the fourth floor (the elevator was usually too crowded); go to the waiting room until time to go to the unit; stand by Gary and talk, as the doctors suggested ("We don't really know what he can hear, so talk as if he can"). So I did. I never had a problem talking, although Gary often said I most certainly did, for I talked too much and shot from the hip too often. I talked about things from our past, funny things, disagreements we had had, which had been few but strong, the children, anything going on at th church, in the community, at my school, in the world. I'm sure often I must have babbled, but I had been known to do that anyway, so he probably just took that in stride.

When my minutes were up, go back to the waiting room. Answer the pay phone in the hall, for so many people were constantly calling. There were no cell phones or other gadgets then, so that phone was all we had. Around noon, go down to the cafeteria and eat dinner. I didn't have much appetite, but I knew I needed to eat. When I had left home that rainy night, Furman Peters and Carolyn Kinard had put cash in my hand, so I was able to buy what I needed. I didn't need much that money could buy, and I had no way to go anywhere (if there had been any place I wanted to go), so my needs were met.

Return to the waiting room and go to the unit at intervals. By 6 p.m. go back to the cafeteria and eat supper. Return to the waiting room and wait. Around 7 p.m. return to the Hospitality House, escorted by a security guard if it was dark by then. The next day, do it all again.

So I lived for a month. One weekend dear friends Cecil and Joyce Bennett brought Carrie Michal to see the dad she would never know.

Where the Wisteria Grows

Amanda came with them. Another weekend a colleague and good friend, Donna McClellan Dodge, brought Garren to Richmond. Donna had gone that summer to the Cataloochee Valley with Gary and me. That was his last camping trip. She and I rode horses while Gary fished. The first weekend in November the church flew me home to be there for our annual Harvest Day service. It was wonderful to see my parents and the children. I gave the church a first-hand, face-to-face report on their pastor. It was a rather strange day – almost surreal. I didn't feel sad, exactly, but I was strongly aware of a void. This was a subconscious awareness, yet, had I been asked, I could have identified it. This was a moment in time like a very few others I have had, when I was in a place, saying and doing things, smiling and touching those I love and who love me, yet feeling that I was somewhere else looking down at myself, as if looking through a scrim where images seem to have a light film over them. It's a feeling of being there, yet not.

Another weekend I took my first real train ride when I went home on Amtrak. James Sease, one of our deacons, picked me up in the nearby town of Denmark. That weekend I spent with our children, whose minds I couldn't quite read, but I knew they were taking their cues from me. Fortunately, for them and me, I have never been a crybaby nor one to fall to pieces first and get things together later. In the wee hours of Sunday morning, James took me back to the train station.

There were others who made the long trip to Richmond, to see Gary, to be with me, to bring me hugs and laughter: Uncle Ray and Aunt Dot, my "other parents," and our Tennessee cousins Beetle and Lillie Mae Strange; Gary's sister Janice; the Drivers, parents of one of my colleagues; a Catholic priest who was a friend of a friend; other pastors and laypeople from the Richmond area whom I did not know and would never see again.

I found myself refreshed and uplifted by all of these people – those who came, as well as those who called. My job was held secure

I was not allowed to feel alone.

Where the Wisteria Grows

When night fell and quiet began to settle, the busyness of the day would fade, and, no matter how loved, secure, and strong I had felt, and no matter how many people may be at the Hospitality House, the bed where I lay and waited for sleep was full of just me and my thoughts.

There are parts of our valleys that are lonesome, and we have to walk them by ourselves. All of the loving people in my life could not walk all of the steps with me, although they would willingly do so. Some things nobody can do for us. As for me, I instinctively put my trust in the hand of the God whose love runs deeper than my needs.

There was no other way.

Where the Wisteria Grows

15
To Charleston

November moved toward its end. The days were warm—the languorous warmth of Indian summer, when the sky is an opaque blue that looks and feels different from the blue sky of summer or any other time of the year. I walked the grounds of the capital. I walked up and down the city streets, block after block, mile after mile. I couldn't constantly stay in the hospital, where I could do nothing but be there and answer that pay phone. So I walked, going nowhere, buying nothing, passing strangers, wondering, praying, nodding occasionally to passers-by, moving in and out of the shadows of buildings, of trees wearing their multi-colored fall finery, walking mile after mile. I felt somewhat like the character in Ray Bradbury's story "The Pedestrian," who, when the faceless police asked, "What are you doing?" the nameless pedestrian replies, "Walking. Just walking."

With Thanksgiving just a week away, I realized we had to go home. We could not stay in Richmond where family wasn't. Meanwhile, Gary was moved from the neuroscience unit to the cardiac unit, a move I discovered when I came in one morning. He was still deep in a coma. I was perplexed and immediately began to ask questions. Soon Dr. Young, surgeon chief of the neurology department, came to me. He explained Gary was stable and the bed in the neurological unit needed to be vacated to make room for other patients. The cardiac unit could do now what needed to be done.

I accepted his explanation. I had no way of knowing what he did not tell me: that this move was an intermediate move toward a "regular" room, out of the trauma wards. Neither did he tell me Gary had staph in his blood, an infection with a 30% mortality rate. He could not tell me when, or if, Gary would ever regain consciousness. He had made that clear from the beginning.

Things now began to look more uncertain than ever, and, for the first time, I felt a small knot of fear begin to form deep inside me. It occurred to me that I had enough to deal with without fear dumping itself into the basket. But there it was.

Phil Bryant had been Gary's close friend since college days. He had been serving as pastor of the French Huguenot Church in Charleston, a curious anomaly Gary and I had discussed. Phil was an ordained Southern Baptist minister, educated in Baptist schools, an only child from a small community not far from Greer, a former gang member, and could no more prove any Huguenot ancestry than our Irish setter. Yet Phil always had "connections," and had a personality that could charm the socks off a snake.

As pastor of that church, he knew and had become friends with some of the oldest families in Charleston.

Shirley Bishop Brown had been born and raised in Ehrhardt. She had moved her way up from floor nurse at the Medical University of South Carolina hospital to supervisor. As a case worker she served as court witness in pediatric and gynecological cases. Her parents were members of our church and had "adopted" us when we first came to Ehrhardt.

So Phil and Shirley were the people I called to help me get Gary to Charleston. I knew they could make it happen.

On the day before Thanksgiving, Gary and I were transported by air ambulance to Charleston. Phil met us at the airport in the cool pre-dawn darkness, where a ground ambulance took Gary on to the hospital where Shirley had made sure everything was ready on "Eye West," the place where she assured me he would get the best care. I left it all to her.

Phil took me on to his house in Summerville.

Where the Wisteria Grows

By the time we arrived, the early streaks of dawn's light were lacing the sky. I went to bed and slept for a few hours. I must have slept soundly, for I did not hear Claudia, Phil's wife, leave for school. Later, Phil took me to the hospital. Shirley met us there.

I looked out of the window of the hospital room, seeing the Cooper River Bridge, the ships moving slowly on the water, the wharves, the narrow streets below, the warehouses and homes that have survived wars, hurricanes, earthquakes, fires. I looked at Gary, attached to machines, and I thought: in this odd place and dark time, we are home. Now I can make my way back to the children and to so much that has defined us, shaped us, and, in some strange way that only God does things, prepared us for such a time as this.

Tomorrow would be Thanksgiving.

Where the Wisteria Grows

16
Thanksgiving

Mother was in my kitchen preparing Thanksgiving dinner. Cousin Judy was there. Her husband Bobby had bought land and an old house about eight miles out of town. This was his "hunting lodge." Friends and relatives from the Upstate came and went during the long deer hunting season. The old house stood several hundred yards from the road, unseen by passers-by. It was an impressive building made of cypress and fat lighter pine, a dark, unpainted structure built in the 19th century. A porch wrapped around the front, and huge, old moss-draped live oaks kept most of the house under their shadow. Bobby had re-wired it, built a beautiful rock fireplace between two of the rooms, cleaned the old wide boards that formed the walls, floors, and doors, and then coated them with polyurethane. The house was perfect for its purpose. So, during deer season, there was always company. Garren honed the hunting and woodsman's skills his dad had already taught him, and he experienced the camaraderie of the men who frequented what I called "the spook house," for it was spooky in its own darkness and shrouded by the moss-covered old oaks. This was good for him. The men were decent, hard-working family guys, most of them churchgoers, patriots, and respectful of children, women, property, and the gifts of the woods, swamps, and wildlife.

So on this warm Lowcountry Thanksgiving day, I was home. The smell of Mother's dressing with its fresh sage filled the house. I awoke alone in the old walnut bed, and I began to feel a wave come over me, building rapidly toward the force of a tsunami.

Mother had gone home for a while. She and Dad had sold the mill village house in '85 and bought a nice, comfortable brick home on a quiet street two blocks from us.

Judy was in the guest bedroom across the hall. Bobby and the boys were at Bobby's "spook house." I made my way to Judy, lay down next to her, and did what I had not yet done: I fell apart, sobbing and shaking uncontrollably. She just held me in her own quiet, gentle way. "Let it all out, girl."

Eventually, I spent myself. I have done that only a few times over the years. Mostly there was just too much to deal with, for life had now acquired the power to become overwhelming, and somehow I realized I could not let it take me.

It was time to trim the wisteria bush, for the roots were rapidly growing and would soon entangle me.

Like Gary, I had too much to live for; there were children to finish raising, and I may very well have to do that alone. I had a job. I had responsibilities, and if I let myself become overwhelmed and allowed myself to fall apart, I would be the loser, and I would not lose alone. My family and especially Gary had to know our lives were not over. I remembered again that the God who had begun a good work in us would be faithful to complete it.

Where the Wisteria Grows

17
Doctors Mike & Daniel

"Hon, something's wrong with your mother," Dad said. I could hear the alarm in his voice. It was December 9. I had been to Charleston that day. The children had come home from school. I left Garren and Seth in charge of Carrie Michal while I rushed down to their house. Mother stood at the kitchen sink. When I got to her side, she looked at me blankly. "Stroke," I thought. Her family was replete with strokes. There was no cancer, no heart disease, no respiratory problems, but strokes. I picked up the phone and did what most of us in Ehrhardt did: I called Daniel Chassereau, the town's only druggist. Daniel was a brilliant man, and was calm and equally effective with dogs, horses, and people. I called the pharmacy. It was 6:10 p.m. He closed at 6. He happened to be there and answered the phone. His employees had left for the day. "Daniel, I think Mother has had a stroke."

"I'm on my way," he said. In less than two minutes, he was at the house and had the blood pressure cuff on Mother. He said, "Call the ambulance." He was calm and controlled, talking gently to Mother, who was still staring blankly. I heard him tell her, "Try to swallow this pill, Mrs. Ruby." At that moment, he broke the law, for the medication he gave her to try to lower her blood pressure was prescription. I would learn later that he couldn't even get a reading on her blood pressure. While the ambulance was on its way, he called our doctor and told him what he had given Mother. "I broke the law," he confessed. Dr. Mike said, "Good. You may have saved her life."

It wouldn't be the first or last life Daniel would help save.

Mother had suffered a cerebral hemorrhage. It would be the first of three over the next few years. She was admitted to the county hospital. Now I found myself going to Charleston one day and the county hospital the next. Judy Bazzle kept children in her home. Hers was the only day care within 15 miles. She, Joyce Bennett, Jennifer Miller, and others in the community shared the care of Carrie Michal, who was now 16 months old.

During this time, the doctors advised me to find a nursing home for Gary; the situation had plateaued and would get no better.

So I did. I went to one facility after another, and each time I was losing whatever grip I had on myself and my life. Neither Gary nor I have ever been subject to depression, but I felt now, during this Christmas season, that I could not go on. After leaving a facility in Branchville, S.C., I came back through Bamberg. I was crying and shaking. I stopped at Dr. Michael Watson's office. I don't know why. The office was closed. The early darkness of December had already fallen. But there I was, getting out of the car that Hallman Sease, our town's only car dealer, had gotten for me. When I was in Richmond, I didn't need a car, but when I came home, it occurred to me that I had nothing to drive except Gary's '88 GMC pickup, and Garren had to drive it to school. So Hallman found a very nice black Oldsmobile '98, and that is what I parked outside of Dr. Mike's. One light was on in the building. I went to it, looked through a window, and there he stood. I knocked on the window. He looked up, saw me, and opened the door. I collapsed in his kind arms, and he just let me "let it go." When I could speak, I garbled, "I can't do this!" I don't remember what he said at that point, if anything, but I do remember hearing, "You have got to get some rest, and sometimes it is all right to take something." I think I pulled away from him, straightened myself, wiped my face with tissue he gave me, and said, "Not yet."

"Call me if you change your mind."

I left him feeling a little less despair. When I got home, there

Where the Wisteria Grows

were cars all around the house. I opened the door, and the house was full of people. My choir had bought and decorated a Christmas tree. (I had neither thought of that nor did I have the heart for it.) They made sure there were gifts under it, and they had brought food. My children had found my decorations and helped create this warm, wonderful surprise, and here I was a basket case. They immediately began to lift me. By the time they left, the basket had begun to re-weave itself.

Despite their efforts, another darkness settled in later in the evening. The children had gone to bed, the food had been stashed in the refrigerator, yet none of that could fill the emptiness and void where Gary and Mother should be. Poor Pop was lost without her; for 56 years she had been his strength, the beauty and wonder in his life, crowning him and his beautiful, loving children with grace and love he never felt he deserved.

Daylight would come in a few hours, and, all around me and throughout the world people would get up, go to work, eat, and take care of theirs. The villagers in Shangpo and Richmond would try to have a daily day, but, like me, that may not happen.

Gary knew nothing.

Where the Wisteria Grows

18
A Room With a View

One thing Charleston has in common with the mountains: to me, both are beautiful no matter the time of year. The city's charm, resiliency, narrow cobbled streets, rainbow houses, smells of salt marsh mingled with the oily odors of the steamers making their way through the harbor and along the wharves – all of these things and more create a languid beauty and agelessness that city leaders work tirelessly to protect. Like its sister city to the south, Savannah, it is an odd blend of the old and the new, past and present, and, like every other place, peopled with the good, the bad, and the ugly – another microcosm of the world. Except in Charleston, as in much of the South, the bad and the ugly tend to have better manners. If a Charlestonian raises his hand to you for harm, he likely will say, "Excuse me" first. The city's heat from mid-April to late September is sultry and oppressive; the rest of the year is comfortably cool. True, cold wind can blow across the waters of the harbor and the Ashley and Cooper Rivers that flow into it, and snow or ice has been known to fall. The winter of 1865 when Sherman worked his way through Georgia and South Carolina was bitterly cold. But most of the time that isn't so. Consequently, there is something blooming almost year round.

For several years, Gary and I had season tickets to the Dock Street Theater. Every spring, we chose one day of Spoleto to attend a chamber concert in the early afternoon and an opera or other theater production in the evening. Between events, we would walk the old streets, taking in free recitals, the work of artists on the sidewalks, and then have dinner at one of the city's many excellent

Where the Wisteria Grows

restaurants. These were our "dates" during the year.

Now our dates were different. Now we met in a hospital room in "Eye West," where his food came through a tube and mine, if I ate, came from the cafeteria downstairs. Now, as far as I or anyone else knew, he never knew I was there, talking, writing, looking out the window, reading – not doing anything much except being there and refusing to believe this is where our story would end.

Many people came and went now that we were closer to home. Someone – maybe Joyce Bennett, maybe Meg Herndon – thought to put a notebook in the room, a registry of those who came during those weeks. Often, however, I sat alone in a room occupied by two of us.

Where the Wisteria Grows

19
Christmas Dinner

For all its color, pageantry, frivolity, serious intent, and tradition, Christmas is so much sadness. Think about it: we Christians, no matter what brand we are, see the birth of The Redeemer, the fulfillment of ancient prophecy, as the Savior of a mankind who, for the most part, does not recognize he has a problem. We have inherited a Holy Word inspired by a God who organizes armies, makes them absolute killing machines, forgives the most unforgivable people, and seems to order the obliteration of innocents, yet calls us to service, obedience to a power we do not understand, and commands us to forgive the dregs of a world inhabited by people to whom he gave a choice.

They messed up, and their offspring do the same. Far be it from me to understand how an omniscient power puts up with so much trash in his creation. Sometimes I think the last thing he should do is plan a second coming to this besotted planet.

If Socrates, Aristotle, St. Augustine, and all of that "great cloud of witnesses" who have gone before us didn't figure all of this out, I would be smart to leave it alone. So, back to Christmas. Most Christians have no clue that most of our "tradition" is saturated with paganism. I would give my students bonus questions on their tests during Advent: Was Jesus born on Dec. 25? How many kings visited the baby Jesus? How many gifts did they present? What is Hanukkah? (A question even fewer got right.) Now, you could say I was unfair with that question, but every chance I got to communicate the relevance of our faith, laws, and customs to the Jewish heritage, I presented the information, and I never felt threatened, off base, or unfair in doing so.

Few got their bonus, even though many of them had grown up in Sunday School, church, Vacation Bible School, etc. If I had tossed the same questions to many other life-long church-goers, too many would have missed the answers. We have been schooled, in the past few generations in America, by Currier and Ives, Hallmark cards, and even Dickens himself.

Mostly all of this has nothing to do with the fact that on Christmas Day, 1990, all of my children and I had Christmas dinner at the Waffle House on Savannah Highway just south of Charleston. We had spent part of the day with their comatose father in Eye West. Did I know how these beautiful children borne from Gary and me felt, or what they were thinking?

No.

I made educated guesses:
(1) This is not the way Christmas is supposed to be.
(2) Mother is supposed to smoke a turkey.
(3) Mimi and Grandpa are supposed to be here.
(4) The meat is here because Dad and Garren made it happen.
(5) There is supposed to be music.
(6) There are so many gifts to be opened.

But they ordered. We, or I, said some kind of blessing. Carrie Michal sat in a booster seat.

On that strange yet warm day, I have never felt more bonded, connected, welded, with these four beautiful people that God, Gary, and I had created. I knew Gary was with us in ways I did not, at the time, realize. I do believe that, in the way only the Omniscient Presence can present, Gary was there in that Waffle House, and I was reminded in the most powerful way God can show that here we are, family, tied by blood, the most powerful force in life, and bound with so many others, some of whom we will never know, by a love that will not let us go.

Where the Wisteria Grows

20
Coming Back

Christmas faded into a past whose lights, tinsel, gifts, and songs disappeared in a box lined with memories and emotions painted in a dull gray. Like so many other Christmases, it left a bittersweetness: warmth, love, kindness, yet a void that only Gary and Mother could fill.

New Year's Day was Mother's birthday. In 1991, she turned 71. Hospital rooms with their sterility and blandness are not the best venue for birthday parties. But Mother was recovering, and, within the next three months, would return to 98% of herself, resuming her care for Dad and Carrie Michal. She would never be as strong, but the lights of love and laughter would remain bright as long as she lived.

Meanwhile, Gary began to awaken. His right eye slowly and sporadically opened, showing signs of recognition. Agitation increased as his mind and body began to resurrect to what must have been a frightening sense of consciousness. On January 7, 1991, he was discharged to HealthSouth Rehabilitation Center in Columbia. He would remain there until April, coming back to life with an intensity and quickness that seemed determined to defy the deep darkness of the past months.

He has no memory of the accident. All he knows about what happened to him is what I have told him. His first words were a question spoken from the hospital bed at HealthSouth: "What happened to Phil?"

I will always wonder what was in his mind when he asked about Phil Bryant. Maybe it was a moment similar to those we have when we are dreaming yet not quite asleep, and people and images take on that surreal sense of suspension of consciousness where nothing is clear.

"Nothing has happened to Phil," I said. He looked bewildered. "You were in a very bad accident. You have been in a coma since October. This is January. We have a long road ahead, but we are traveling, and we will make it."

I could read the confusion on his face as he tried to process this. It was then, for the first time, I saw a tear form in his left eye. His right eye stayed mostly closed and would remain that way until March of '92 when he would have double surgery on it — one procedure to open it and another to do a muscle tuck. He would never again have much vision in that eye.

I went back to my classroom on January 8, to the children I had just gotten to know when the accident happened. They were kind and asked often how things were going for us. There were hugs and more hugs. My colleagues — indeed, the entire school and school district — stood by us, sending cards (one signed by all of Tessie Jo Morris's students), calling, giving money to the Gary Mullinax fund. I have kept a box with stacks of cards, many hand-made by my middle schoolers. My job was held for me. I was never threatened with its loss, nor was my pay ever docked. Moreover, when I had exhausted my days, the district loaned me more.

Every other day I would leave when school was out and drive to Columbia. Gary's progress was phenomenal, as he responded strongly to therapy. He would become a therapist's dream, for he was determined, increasingly strong, never afraid, and he never whined.

Mother left the hospital in early January and went to Rita Kay's. Mother also responded well to therapy, for, like Gary, she was determined, and she was not one to whine. Because of her age, she did not have the physical strength Gary had, but she worked. In April she went home.

The last few weeks at HealthSouth found Gary in therapy six hours a day. I will never forget the day his parents and I walked into the gym and saw him up and moving between parallel bars. When he saw us, his face spread into a wide grin that seemed to say, like an excited child, "Just watch me!"

We all cried.

The winter months gave way to spring. Gary had become a picture of strength and good health. As his discharge grew imminent, some of the men from the church put a ramp up the back steps of the parsonage. When we came home on April 12, Seth's 11th birthday, a large welcoming committee filled the house, yard, and driveway. "This is the best birthday present ever!" Seth exclaimed.

21
A Matter of Time

In English grammar, the simple past tense of a verb indicates an action that was completed in the past. There is no recurring action in this tense. The action is complete. Finished. As in, "I ate my supper." The food may not all be gone, but I have finished the act of eating.

There are three simple tenses in the active voice of verbs. They are aptly called "simple": the simple present ("I see you"), the simple past ("I saw you"), and the simple future ("I will see you"). The simple present means that, from time to time, or regularly, I see you. The simple past indicates a completed action. The simple future – well, I think it explains itself.

Then there are the "perfect" tenses: present perfect, past perfect, and future perfect. Don't ask me who laid down these rules; it was my job to teach the grammar. I spent years trying to explain and model this "standard book" English, to who knows how many kids who spoke a dialect that meshed African, southern, some old English, and who knows what else besides just "bad" grammar. As the years went by, I cared less about how they spoke, but I cared more that, when placed in a job interview, or sitting down to complete an application, or meeting people in arenas where they might want to place themselves, they would make the rules work for them. I know most of us choose our methods of communication according to our immediate audience. When I am with my mountain neighbors, family, professionals, and close friends, my speech and mannerisms quickly find their place. This has nothing to do with "putting on airs" or switching to non-standard English. It has everything to do with communication.

We make these adjustments subconsciously most of the time. Within each of us is the embedded language, and we often say more when we say less.

So it was that I had no problem communicating with all of the medical community with whom I now had contact. I began to make transitions from the rehabilitation climate to my seventh-grade classroom to my neighbors in the small town in which we lived, and to family. That is not to say I always understood all of the jargon, but I learned to persist until I understood.

Oddly, 20 years later, after constant caregiving, after becoming a grandmother and retiree, I learned new meanings for those verb tenses I had taught for so long.

(a) Gary had a head injury. There was the accident, his head was injured, and the accident and initial injury were over.

(b) Gary has had a head injury. That is the present perfect tense, indicating that an action occurred in the past and possibly continues to the present. Think of it this way: if you say, "He has always been a hard worker," does that mean someone worked hard and quit? Maybe. But it implies that, although he worked hard, he may continue to do so. It refers to an action that was done in the past but may continue into the present.

(c) A head injury is never over. "Is" is the simple present of the "be" verb, the strangest verb in our language. It indicates an ongoing or recurring state of being. I have concluded that "was" never happens with a head injury. There is always residue: short term memory loss, impaired mental processing, usually physical impairments. And those are the brighter sides. For many there are mood swings, seizures, health issues, early onset of more debilitating memory issues like dementia and Alzheimer's.

Considering all of that, we were blessed. Gary got up. Although he had no use of his right hand and arm and little use of the lower right side of his body, he got up. He worked at living and being the servant

Where the Wisteria Grows

his heart commanded him to be.

He was in and out of outpatient rehab for years. During May and June of '91, his Dad and others took him several times a week to Orangeburg for therapy. When school was out in June, I traveled up and down the road bordered by the black-water cypress swamps he loved.

In some strange way, our lives found a new normalcy. In the summer of '92 he resigned from the pastorate at Ehrhardt. Twenty years had passed since the hot August when we arrived in that small town. Our lives had become ensconced in this Lowcountry community founded by German immigrants more than 100 years earlier. Our children were born and grew up here, where Gary had served as buffer and de-fuser, at times, of any number of scandals, and consistently stood firm with integrity, humility, and wisdom.

Now it was time to move. I had to find us a place to live. Because of his uncanny foresight, that was not as difficult as it could have been. In the late 80s, despite my vociferous objections, he borrowed money and bought the lot next to my parents. At the time, the last thing I wanted was property in Ehrhardt. I had begun to think our work was mostly done, and we needed to move on.

I still didn't know much.

We had rented the lot to Mary Ann Wilson. The lot already had a septic tank and municipal water. She moved a single-wide mobile home there and became a quiet, friendly neighbor to my parents. Gary had bought part of a large section of a shed from the former Clayton poultry farm. He could get it for one price if the Claytons tore it down, or much less if he tore it down – which he did. He put it down behind Mother's. Gary put a pump on the well that the original homeowner had dug but never used, and he housed it in what had been Amanda's playhouse. The shed went over it all, and there we parked the used Winnebago we had bought in '86, the horse trailer, and any number of other things that just find their way into sheds and barns.

Where the Wisteria Grows

When we needed to move, Mary Ann graciously moved her home to another location. Through Gary's cousin Ricky Mullinax, who worked for Kent-Gault Mobile Homes in Greenville, we were able to get a very nice four-bedroom, three-bath double wide which Ricky set up on the lot. He installed the air conditioner, and he made sure everything was done right. Mullinax men are like that. Do things right or not at all.

On a rainy Labor Day weekend in September, 1992, we moved in. The church had allowed us to live in the parsonage and had paid Gary's salary until then.

Another page of our lives had turned, and there was no way to know what lay ahead. All I could do at the moment was give thanks with a grateful heart.

Where the Wisteria Grows

Mother and Dad – 1984,
Spring Street, Woodside

Bee man

70s selfie – fire tower in
Cataloochee

1975, Cataloochee Valley

Barry, Rita, Renee – 1978

All in the family

Relaxing at Edisto

Gary and Carrie Michal, September, 1989

*Carrie Michal at Amanda's
wedding*

Rev. Mullinax

Sisters: Amanda and Carrie Michal on Buttermilk

April, 1991 – Gary comes back home

School picture –
Ehrhardt Elementary, 1998

Sadie and me
Winter '08-'09 The Glade

"Closer to Heaven"

"Closer to Heaven" with
Sadie and Bootleg

Garren's high school graduation, 1992

Family Picture - August 16, 2014

22
Going to School

Ann Gallop lived on a farm about eight miles out of town. She was our organist. She was also a fine kindergarten teacher who helped prepare all our children to read. She came to Gary in the early 90's and asked him about volunteering at the elementary school just a few blocks away. During the 90's Gary was able to move about the house with the aid of a hemi-walker. It was unnerving to watch him, as his right leg, like the whole right side of his body, was barely functional due to semi-paresis. I had bought a golf cart, and he managed to get himself outside to the bottom of the steps where the cart was, get in, and go about in the small community. Since there was no home delivery of mail in town, everyone went to the post office to get the mail. There was also a bank in town. Every day Gary would drive the few blocks to the post office, or go to the bank if I had a deposit to make. Everyone knew him and helped. Every other day he went to Junior's barber shop across from the bank, where the men who killed part of every morning at Junior's helped him in and Junior gave him a shave.

However, for whatever reason, he didn't immediately go to the school. He had taught school in New Orleans, and he was a gifted teacher. Ann soon retired, and Diana Varn, another resident of the community, began teaching at the school. Diana had grown up just a few miles from Ehrhardt. She had married a local businessman and had been teaching for a few years already. She approached Gary about helping at the school. This time he went. Thus began a beautiful, productive relationship that would last for more than 10 years.

Gary would make his way out of the house and drive to the school where one of the children would bring a wheelchair to the little cart. He would get in the chair, go to Diana's classroom, and the children would take turns reading to him. The staff in the small lunchroom would fix his lunch and put it in a plastic bag that he could carry home. He would take treats and dispense them to the children who read their passage without missing a word. A loving bond grew among him, the children, and the staff, most of whom lived in the community. Indeed, he had been pastor to a number of them.

He considered himself the greatest beneficiary in this work. He had found "something to do," and it was something he did faithfully and with the tireless unselfishness he had given his ministry. For him, this was ministry, enabling him to continue in some way that to which he had been called and for which he had lived.

In 1996 he was the Christmas parade marshal. He drove the little cart and pulled a wagon full of schoolchildren down the little main street. The wagon had been royally and painstakingly decorated by Charlotte, with the help of Ginger Ellis.

A few years later the governor of South Carolina awarded Gary the Order of the Silver Crescent for his work with the school. This beautiful document hung on the wall of his room with other awards and recognitions, most of which he earned since an accident that would have rendered lesser men and women useless and empty. There is recognition for outstanding service to the Bamberg County Department of Social Services (DSS), awarded by the S.C. Legislature in '92; the plaque given in '97 by the county DSS; a large, framed copy of the article written about him and published in *The State*, South Carolina's largest newspaper; the certificate of appreciation for the volunteer work he did at Barnwell Elementary School after we moved to Barnwell in '04.

Over the years, he has officiated at a number of funerals and weddings, including the marriages of Amanda and Garren. In '91 he baptized Seth, who had made a commitment to God just before the accident. He sat in a chair by the baptismal pool and said the words of institution. In '98 he baptized Carrie Michal, saying the words of institution while our pastor, Charlie Barnard, did the "dunking."

To the children who grew up under his ministry, he is the only pastor most of them consider they will ever have. He set a standard of walking in honesty and wisdom, never violating a trust or confidence. He baptized many of them into a faith that they saw him live.

They have not forgotten.

23
Dirty Windows, Streaked Glass

I can't stand dirty windows. I've been known to stand out-side in the snow and clean the four sliding-glass double doors that face the northwest side of our house. Every place we have lived, my custom was to clean windows, blinds, window dressings and sills the first week after school was out. If Vacation Bible School was that first week (which it was as long as I was director, which was a long time), the window cleaning fell into the next week. The parsonage was large – around 2,000 square feet, and the year we moved there the church had installed storm windows, which I pulled out and cleaned; the screens came out and I hosed them, remov-ing months of accumulated dust and dirt. The cheap curtains I had bought were washed and ironed, window sills were washed with Clorox water. I have moved every piece of furniture we have ever owned, including the antique walnut armoire with long beveled mirrors that Gary bought in New Orleans in '71. When we moved into the double wide, I cleaned windows, but it was easier because the windows were the newer tilt windows that could be cleaned inside and out without ever having to go outside and get on a ladder.

Now if you ask me why I have this "fetish," as some would say, I have a number of answers.

(1) Mother cleaned windows at least once a year in the old mill house where there were definitely no storm windows (who ever heard of such?), and someone definitely had to get on a serious ladder to do the outside. She also ironed the lacy scarves the lamps sat on.

(2) I want to see the outside and feel the light of day, the cleanness of sunshine.

(3) I want to see a clear day unmarked by streaks, film, or fingerprints on the only thing between me and out there. As much as I am awed by the glorious sunsets here on the mountain, they reveal to my eyes all of the places I missed when I was cleaning the doors and windows. Sometimes they just drive me to grab the nearby glass cleaner and cloths or paper towels and rub and wipe until the sun goes behind Crabtree Mountain and takes the marred places on my windows and doors with it.

Now I am not deceived. I know perfectly well tomorrow's afternoon sun will mock me. "Ha, ya think ya got it all, doncha? Look, look, look!" So like a dummy, I look, seeing what I already knew was there, and I can't stand it.

Then I think of what Lavinia Bishop said not long after we moved to Ehrhardt: "It's a small town, and everybody lives on one side or the other of the glass."

I decided I had a new reason to keep the glass as clean as possible. You may not know what goes on behind closed doors, but, if you look, you can see what is behind the glass, and the cleaner the glass is, the better the picture.

So I keep cleaning the glass, one way or the other. I've never been able to find anything that completely removes the prints, the film, the streaks. And, believe me, I've tried everything short of just doing away with the glass.

In '92 Garren graduated from Bamberg-Ehrhardt High School. He had a part-time job at a local hardware store. He was a tall, handsome, blue-eyed young man, congenial, respected – a guy who, as his friend Alex told me years later, "was always different." I knew what Alex meant: Garren played by the rules. To this day, I wonder what went on in his mind when his dad left our lives in so many ways. Yet he didn't seem to know which way to go. He moved to Columbia for a while, went to school for a while, and, finally,

Where the Wisteria Grows

chose to join the Navy. "Mama, do you think I've made the right choice?" It took me a while to answer, but I finally said, "Do it." One of the hardest moments in my life was the Sunday morning when Gary, Carrie Michal, Seth and I drove to Orangeburg to the bus station and I watched my tall, beautiful son get on a bus and go away.

Of course, the moment, difficult as it was, pales compared to the years before and since when mothers sent their children to battlefields, strange lands, and into conflicts that powers with both named and nameless faces created in the name of conquest, ambition, control, and, always, money.

In '94, Amanda graduated magna cum laude from the University of South Carolina. One week later, she married a wonderful man, a believer who, like her dad, desired what was best for her, and continues to hold her in the highest respect and honor.

Exactly one week later, my dad died, mostly of old age.

Six weeks later Gary's dad died after a battle with emphysema.

In October, Carrie Michal came home from kindergarten and found Mother on the kitchen floor of her house. She had suffered a second cerebral hemorrhage. Carrie Michal ran to a neighbor's, Darlene Kay, who called the ambulance. Then Darlene called me at school. I went straight to the hospital.

Another streak in the glass. This time the glass cleaner and paper towels were useless.

Where the Wisteria Grows

24
Dust

Someone told me recently the biggest component of dust is dead skin. When I was growing up on the mill village our neighbor Blanche referred to the "dead men" under the furniture. My cousin Dottie Rae talks about dust bunnies everywhere in her house, which is totally not true as she has the cleanest house of anybody I know of since Phylis Hiers was alive. She was one of our church members, and her husband Claude had to take off his shoes at the back door.

Dust bunnies, dead men, dead skin – I don't like dust. It's another one of life's annoyances, like a streak in the glass that makes itself known when light is the brightest. Here on the mountain, that's in the afternoon and early evening when the sun has made its way to the west side of the house and throws its merciless cleanness through these four glass double doors. The piano I thought was so clean, the wood floors I had so meticulously vacuumed and mopped, the long kitchen table Gary made years ago and that I just cleaned – all wearing dust. Sometimes I grab the Pledge and dust cloth and work in a frenzy while the sun is still showing me everything I thought was gone. It's a losing battle. While my back is turned, the dead men/dead skin/dust bunnies are proliferating, like germs on unwashed hands.

Like troubles and crises in our lives, bulging and bullying their way like the roots of wisteria.

Amanda, like her dad, has always been a vociferous reader and writer. When she was 15 years old she was chosen for the South Carolina Governor's School for the Arts, a five-week intensive summer program for the visual and performing arts.

She went for the writing program. The school was then held on the beautiful campus of Furman University in Greenville, S.C. Gary went there every summer for the Furman Pastor's School. I took her the day she began this course of study, and when she got out of our Volkswagen Rabbit that she hated, I watched her walk away, a tiny girl, the first of the four beautiful gifts God had blessed us with, and I felt such a sense of desolation and loss. She had come to this strange place where she knew no one, where she would find herself surrounded by some of the brightest and best of her peers, kids from all corners of the Palmetto State, many of them troubled and even more of them eccentric in their own artistic ways. We were so proud of her, for this was a great honor and opportunity, one behind which her teachers, our family and community threw their prayers and full support.

So why did I have these negative feelings, so much like the ones I had later when Garren got on that bus in Orangeburg?

I am not sure. I am fairly sure I had these feelings for different reasons. With Amanda on that hot summer day, somehow I knew our lives and our relationship would never be the same. We would remain strong and devoted to each other, but she was entering a different world, moving away from childhood, taking a giant step toward the woman she would become: confident, bright, compassionate, honest to a fault, and driven to work toward the mark of the High Calling God had been revealing to her all of her life. When we left home that day, Gary said to her, "Always remember who you are."

"The preacher's daughter," she said.

"You are the King's daughter," he replied.

At that moment in our lives, there seemed to be no dust or streaks. At least not the kind we would come to know later.

By the time Garren left for the Navy, we had experienced much, and when he boarded the bus that day, the feelings that took me came with the realization that loss is what life gives us.

Where the Wisteria Grows

Then when we are hit by silent hurricanes, we and those around us can exercise the faith we have purported, and it becomes a living, breathing part of us, pulsing with its own intense energy. We may have lost, but during the losing, we are gaining.

25
Tides of Life?

When Cousin Judy's boys were in their late teens, they started bull riding. Such daring-do was not inherited from their parents, although Judy played aggressive basketball in high school, and Bobby had his own competitive edge. But bull riding? I asked Bobby once why he thought Brad and Jeff took up such a life-threatening activity. "I don't know," he said, shaking his head. "They musta got mixed up in the hospital when they were born."

Sometimes our children turn on us that way, pursuing the call of insanity, knowing their parents will die another day every time they get on that raging bull, or, in Seth's case, get on that high bar or mat in a gym.

Seth's natural physical ability was in gymnastics. He started when he was eight years old. Gary had already noticed the spring in Seth's legs and his utter fearlessness. There was no gym within 40 miles of Ehrhardt, and that one did not have a strong boys' program. Ultimately, he left home when he was 15 and went into training with Dan and Dennis Hayden. They were former aspiring Olympians, but, due to injuries, left the mats and bars and came to Augusta, Ga., where they opened their own gym and had an up-and-coming boys' program. Seth boarded first with our friends the Timmermans in Aiken, S.C., and commuted to the gym with some other boys. When he was old enough to drive, he moved to Augusta and boarded with one of his teammates and his mother.

During meet season, we hit the road: Atlanta, Greenville, Knoxville, Chattanooga, Tampa, Houston. I'd load Gary, the wheelchair, and sometimes Carrie Michal, travel, sit in the gym or civic center for hours and hours, and I would hold my breath or close my eyes when Seth got to the high bar, the rings, or any other event. He developed that sleek, subtle strength gymnasts have. It is different from the mass and bulk football players pursue. It is more like the power and grace of a ballet dancer.

The kind of fear and anxiety a parent feels in this situation is not like the same feelings we have when the events of life take us to the back of a bull or the reach of the high bar. As the 90s swept by, each year was marked by loss and change. Much of what happened was supposed to happen, for it fell within the natural ebb and flow of life. Mother's brother Milton died, as did Uncle Ben; Uncle Ray died of cancer just a few short years after he retired. In '97, Mother suffered a third cerebral hemorrhage. She lingered quietly and was unresponsive for almost two weeks, and then she died. When that happened, Gary cried, for he and Mother had always been soulmates.

I had gotten to the age where death comes more often.

Other things ran against the normal tides of life. In August of '96, just before school started, Gary began projectile vomiting. He didn't feel bad, but he could not even keep down a saltine cracker. Fearing dehydration, I called the ambulance to take him to the county hospital. A short while after he got there, he was transported to Charleston. For days he endured test after test that showed nothing. On the fourth day, the doctors did an endoscopy. Within hours, Gary was writhing in pain. The doctors were giving him morphine every 15 minutes until they finally moved him to critical care. Amanda sat with me in the waiting room. Around midnight, a doctor called us into an office in the unit. "Acid has seeped into one of his lungs. We cannot operate. He will either get better, or it will spread to his other lung..."

A short while after that, the doctor decided to do one more scan, which Gary was in no condition to withstand. At the last moment, a radiologist said, "Wait. I see something in his chest."

Where the Wisteria Grows

Around 3 a.m., I saw the doctor outside the waiting room. He had on scrubs and had a surgical mask hung around his neck. Amanda and I rushed out into the hall.

"We have found part of his colon in his chest. It has ruptured and put him in septic shock," the doctor explained. "But," he continued, "we can fix this. He will have a temporary colostomy, and then we can put him back together."

Later, when Gary was in recovery, the doctor came to us. "He is stable but weak. We took 12 inches of colon out of his chest." I wanted to know how that happened. It sounded too much like a warped Jack-and-the-beanstalk tale. But I didn't ask at the time. Amanda and I were so ecstatic and relieved, I figured I could ask more questions later.

One cause for this bizarre situation stemmed directly from the accident in '90. At that time, Gary's diaphragm was perforated. Because it is hidden behind the liver, a very large organ, the tear had never been detected. During the following years, the colon had wormed its way into the chest. The theory was that, when the endoscopy was done, the colon tissue tore, allowing the body's sewerage to leak.

Now I had to learn how to manage a colostomy. Rita Kay and I had already learned how to give blood-thinner shots to Mother, so what was a colostomy, except worse smelling? We came home in early September. I went back to school, where Jerry Bell, one of my colleagues, announced, "We've put a new name on your box in the office: Job."

Meanwhile, we were making wedding plans. Garren and Aleathea had set their wedding date in December. Her father was school superintendent in Orangeburg County, and her mother was a speech pathologist for Bamberg District One. We had known them for years – fine Christian people, true, and honest. Garren and Aleathea had finished high school together. Like Amanda's and Daniel's union, we felt secure in our children's choices and proud they had sought and found God's choice for them.

Where the Wisteria Grows

Never mind that he was stationed in San Diego, would come home to get married and have a short honeymoon, then return to California.

Love does not always have the best sense of timing.

Gary was "put back together" a week before the wedding. He was able to do the ceremony, as he had done Amanda's. Mother was able to be there, looking, as my friend Karen said, "like a million dollars," and we worshiped and celebrated as these two beautiful young adults committed themselves to God and each other on a December night in a church lit with candles, poinsettias, and gentle beauty.

Once again I felt the binding of a love that will not let us go.

26
Significance

There are reasons some politicians are loved and reelected term after term. Ted Kennedy of Massachusetts and Strom Thurmond of South Carolina were such people. Thurmond served as governor and later as a senator. He spent most of the 20th century as a public servant.

Kennedy made sure birthdays, anniversaries, graduations, weddings, tragedies and losses, and other important occasions in the lives of his constituents were acknowledged. He could be counted on to step in with his power and presence when his people needed help. To Kennedy, people were important, and they knew this because he paid attention. Granted, a fair amount of this is just political smarts. Point is, people like to feel significant, and they feel this way when someone has time for them and shows them some acknowledgment of their presence.

Same thing with Thurmond. South Carolinians knew if they needed help, Thurmond was the man to get it. He blazed a colorful path across the decades, supporting segregation, then, later, fighting for civil rights, marrying a former Miss South Carolina 30 years his junior after his first wife died, fathering several children, fighting the unionization of textile workers during the early 50s (a sin for which my father never forgave him), a staunch advocate of a strong military, and getting reelected and serving until he died at the age of 100. During his long career, no town or crossroads in South Carolina was too small, no parade too insignificant, no person too unimportant for him to give attention.

So it was Senator Thurmond whom we contacted to help bring Garren home in February of '97. Mother had suffered a third cerebral hemorrhage, and we knew this was the last one. She lay still and co-matose in the county hospital.

Sometimes a mother needs her oldest son to lean on. Strom Thurmond helped me have that pillar. Garren arrived from California the day before Mother died. Carrie Michal, seven years old now, was with friend and neighbor Jennifer Miller.

Rita and our dear friend Charlotte, who had helped me with Mother and Gary, were by the bedside. I had gone home to try to rest and actually had the best night's sleep I had had in a long time. When the phone rang at 5 a.m., I knew Mother had died.

She was at peace, and so was I. Barry, Rita, and I did the ser-vice. Gary cried briefly, painful, hard tears. He loved my Mother; she was his fishing buddy and she was always ready to laugh. Theirs was a unique bond.

The last year she lived, I cared for her and Gary. Charlotte stayed with them while I was at school.

I have often been asked, "How did you do it?" My honest an-swer has always been this: when the people you care for are kind, don't whine, laugh often, try to do for themselves, continue to want what is best for you, and genuinely appreciate what you do for them, caring for them becomes a pleasure, an act of joy. They made me feel significant.

I believe the quality of care and the attitude of the caregiver has as much to do with the person receiving the care as it does with the caregiver. For me, caring for people with the grace and true love of my Mother and husband had become an expression of honorable service for which I have no regrets.

At the age of 47, I felt ready to face the days and years ahead. I realized God had been busy equipping me with tools that would help me survive. He had been pruning. Mother and Dad were gone, and, in many ways, so was Gary – here yet gone.

They had given me skills and a resilience as long as they were able. I still had two young children, a job, so much responsibility. Despite all I had learned, I would learn much more.

I was not afraid. For all of the dark days that were behind me, I could see ahead. I couldn't see the details. That was a blessing, for much lay out there in the tomorrows yet to come. Many more dark days. But I had learned darkness doesn't last forever.

Neither does the present.

Where the Wisteria Grows

27
Storms

I have lived through three hurricanes up close: Camille, in 1969, two weeks after we were married and had moved to New Orleans; David, in 1979, when I was teaching at Denmark-Olar High School; and Hugo, which hit the S.C. coast in September of '89. I had said after Camille, "Thank you, I've had enough. I don't need to do this again."

Since when does Mother Nature pay attention to us mortal peons? Carrie Michal was due as Hugo bore down on the southeastern coast. Charleston was in the bull's eye, so to speak. We were only 60 miles inland from Charleston, surrounded by cypress swamps and low lands. I was full-term and ready.

My wonderful nurse midwife, Leigh Wood, said, "We'd better get this show on the road. Be here at the birthing center at six."

Yeah, right, I thought. There's only one slight problem: a major hurricane is knocking on the door.

I had been swimming that day at a private pool owned by a group of citizens in the area. Fortunately, the pool was way out in the country where few people went except those who lived in the area. I didn't worry about someone seeing me floating big-belly up in that pool all by myself.

Around 5:30 Gary and I got in the pickup to go to Bamberg and have our fourth baby. Gary picked up his chainsaw. One of the neighborhood boys, Brandon Sease, whose father was a deacon, asked, "Mr. Gary, you gonna cut the cord with that chainsaw??"

"Never know what may happen tonight."

What did happen was Hugo. Leigh induced labor. I'd never

Where the Wisteria Grows

had that done before. Having babies was too easy for me. As Mammy said to Scarlett, "It's embarrassin', you havin' babies like a fiel' hand." Dummy me didn't know I could ask for pain medication. I just walked the floor pulling that drip machine, looking occasionally at Gary as he sat quietly reading a book. The wind howled outside like a screaming Banshee. Shortly before midnight, the power went out, the generators came on, and Carrie Michal came out.

Gary went home about daylight, and, sure enough, had to cut a path across Lemon Swamp.

Thirteen months later he would leave us.

Not too long ago, Carrie Michal said, during some conversation we were having, "Mama, you didn't raise me." She didn't say it judgmentally. She seemed to just be stating a simple fact.

"Then who did?" I asked, somewhat defensively.

"Mimi. Mrs. Jennifer. Mama Joyce. Lots of people."

She was more right than I wanted to admit.

Thank God in his mercy for all of those wonderful mothers who were there when I wasn't.

Gerald O'Hara referred to Emma Slattery's "poor, fatherless brats," but little of that fit our picture. First, we had no "brats." Second, our children were not fatherless.

Neither were we rich. That part applies.

Carrie Michal lost a father before she could ever know him. The older children, when they talk about the years B.A. (before the accident), describe a life and father she has never known. Moreover, she lost my mother, the mainstay she had had when I was gone.

By the time she was born, Gary had mellowed, a condition which age will usually provide. He called her "my precious child," and would rock her and sit up at night with her. I have a priceless photo of him sitting on the couch on a Sunday afternoon, still in his white shirt and loosened tie, sprawled on the couch with her on his shoulder, and both of them peacefully asleep.

I have often wondered what I could have done differently for

Where the Wisteria Grows

this child who lost so much before she even knew she had it.
I have found no answers that would make any difference.

28
Another Injury

Most of us have more than one life-changing event, if we live long enough. Marriage is such an event, along with bringing children into our lives. We lose parents, grandparents, sometimes a child. Some of these changes are normal, happening in the natural ebb and flow of life. Other events don't fall within the natural order of things. That accident on a messy road in Virginia on an October day in 1990 was such an event, creating trauma and such a dramatic and irreversible change in our lives we would always be colored by it. The reverberations and residue are as persistent and omnipresent as Blanche's dead men, Dottie's dust bunnies, and film streaks on windows.

We had joined the church in Bamberg in the summer of '97. Charlie and Teresa Barnard, native Tennesseans, had come to serve that church in the mid-90s. They were a team, reminding me of the way Gary and I had always worked together. Teresa was very musical and full of appealing personality. Charlie was a salesman – an immensely effective one, too. He could, as the saying goes, sell shoes to a snake. People don't always think of pastors as salespeople, but they very much are just that, and the better they are at it, the more successful they are likely to be. Under Charlie's leadership, churches grew. Indeed, there is something to sell, and that product is, if you will, a life-changing, direction-switching commitment to God, worship of Him, and service to others through Him. Like fellow staff member Alton McCollum, Charlie had the gift of encouragement and the ability to make a person believe in himself. Charlie could sell ideas, too, and he had more of them than Carter has liver pills.

So it was to this church we had come after Mother died. It wasn't that far – 15 miles. The church was an old, large brick building that occupied one corner. The United Methodists sat on the next corner. Charlie's sermons were highly creative and never shallow. He was unafraid and honest in the pulpit. Alton McCollum fed music to my soul, a change I needed, for I had been doing the feeding for many years. Teresa and I clicked, as people sometimes do when they meet and instinctively have an affinity with each other.

On December 7, 2003, we came home from church. I pulled close to the steps so I could help Gary get out and onto the porch where his hemi-walker was. "Now, don't try to go up the steps without me." I bounced up the few steps so I could unlock the door – a habit I had developed only recently. At the parsonage, we rarely could even find the door key. Before I could unlock and open the door, Gary had attempted the first step and missed. He fell hard to the cement walkway.

He was hurt. I knew, because he was groaning. I couldn't get him up. I jumped in the golf cart and raced two blocks to the Ehrhardt Church. They were still in session; Gary and I had gone to the early service in Bamberg. I eased the door open. Benny Hughes was the first person I could tap who was young enough and strong enough to help. He followed me home and managed to get Gary into the wheelchair. Then I called 911.

He had broken a hip. Replacement surgery and rehab would become part of our lives again. This time we would be closer – Orangeburg.

And this time the hemi-walker was made history. He would live the rest of his life from a wheelchair.

Where the Wisteria Grows

29
Moving

Not long after Mother died we put the Ehrhardt house on the market. There it would stay for most of the next seven years. In a rural Lowcountry town with a population of approximately 450, there were few lookers. Without jobs and schools (the tiny school in town would close within the next few years, and the high school was 15 miles away in the county seat), people have little interest in settling in such a small community. I continued to drive the 50-mile round trip to Barnwell, taking Carrie Michal with me when she reached second grade. All of the children had gone to school with me after they went through Ann Gallop's kindergarten.

For a few years another rather quiet lull settled over us, creating again our own brand of normalcy. Until Gary broke his hip, he continued going to the school, picking up the mail, getting a shave at Junior's, and generally feeling and being productive.

In September of '04, the house finally sold to one of Mookie Wilson's sisters. Mookie was an Ehrhardt native, born into a large family that lived not too far down the street from us. Mookie had made it to pro baseball. This younger sister worked for the local bank.

I quickly had to find us a place to live in Barnwell. As in so many times in the past, God worked rapidly. I found a nice brick rancher in a quiet neighborhood in town in one of those developments that had sprung up during the 50s, 60s, and early 70s to accommodate the thousands of people who had migrated to the jobs offered by the sprawling Savannah River Site.

The house had been built in the 70s, but it had been well cared for. The owner had died. We made an offer on the house, it was

Where the Wisteria Grows

accepted, and, in less than a month, we had sold, bought, and moved from the little farm community that had been our home for 32 years.

As in all decisions, Gary and I worked in total agreement. I would never have packed the first box if he had had any reservations. Our marriage had been one of "together": there was no "his money" or "her money." Moves we made, things we bought – there were no secrets. There was discussion and serious consideration of "what ifs" and weighing of options. However, the final decision was ours.

An exception to that occurred in December of '88, when he took Amanda and Garren with him to Charleston and returned in a brand new GMC pickup. I was furious!

Another time was in 1987, when he wanted to buy the lot next to my parents. We had talked all of our married lives about returning to the mountains, and more property was a most unwelcome encumbrance.

He bought it anyway.

Good thing, for when he got hurt and we had to move out of the parsonage, we had a place to go.

Before the accident, I had no problem deferring to him, but after he was hurt, I had to learn to take the lead. In recent years, as his deficits have rendered his judgment less solid, I have had to make decisions, but he has been informed every step of the way, even when he forgot most of what we talked about.

Our thinking this time was this: a house in Barnwell would be more marketable, and, since Carrie Michal was entering high school, in a few years she would graduate, I could retire and we could move to our beloved mountains.

This was our sixth move since we had married. I had grown up in the same house on the same mill village and gone from first grade through high school with the same kids I had known all of my life. People I knew didn't move. Gary, however, went to five different high schools as his father followed construction work. He was no stranger to new places, and he had confidence and made necessary adjustments quickly. I had to learn.

Moving is tedious and arduous. We Americans accumulate too much stuff that should have been thrown away, recycled, sold, given away, or burned, but we keep it until we move, and then we have to move it or delete it. And I am not a hoarder by any stretch of the imagination.

Yet I have learned that moving isn't such a big deal when you have the immeasurable, immovable treasures of life that are part of who you are. They travel with you, unseen and unboxed, and they sustain and enable you to be at home no matter where you are.

30
A Temporary Normal

Although the house in Barnwell was structurally sound, it was dark and uninviting inside, bearing the residue of styles popular in the 60s and early 70s. We did extensive work: The children painted most of the rooms, beginning with the dark paneling so typical of the early 70s. Then we removed the old carpet (carpet and wheelchairs make contentious pairs; besides, I hate carpet), and remodeled the tiny half bath. The original parts of the house had lovely hardwood floors that had been well cared for by the previous owners. We added a bay window in the small dinette just off the kitchen. There had been no windows in that area or the kitchen, areas which were separated only by a counter and cabinets. Now we could look out at the pool which a previous owner had built. It had had no attention for a long time, so it took a local pool servicer to clean it and make it usable.

I had a lot of good help, so I only had to take off one day from school. We began the settling in process, which, in many ways, was made easier because I had developed such a network of friends in the community. Except for the one semester in 1979 that I taught at Denmark-Olar High School right after I finished my undergraduate work, I had spent my entire career in Barnwell District 45. For years, that district was the biggest employer in the county, yet we were family. We stood by each other, much in the same way that Lavinia Bishop had described Ehrhardt so many years ago. I had been there long enough to be teaching the children of the first children I came to know in the early 80s.

So the adjustment was smooth. I had transferred to the high school in '03, and, after 22 years in the seventh grade, had my own adjustments to make, but I learned. I had been trained in secondary education, but I had only spent one semester at that level before going to work in Barnwell. Carrie Michal entered the ninth grade. The next year she moved to Columbia and lived with Amanda, spending her sophomore year at Dreher High School. The large school offered much that she needed and wanted. Like Amanda, her interests lay in the arts: reading, music, writing. At the end of that year, Amanda and Daniel moved to San Francisco to attend seminary. Carrie Michal came back home. The next two years were difficult for her, in many ways, for she, like Amanda, felt "different" – not comfortable with the small town social scene and never part of "the crowd."

But we made it.

Gary picked up his volunteer work at Barnwell Elementary School. Gladys Ray, who stayed with him during the day, would take him to the school, where he worked with our dear friend from seminary days, Sharon Warren.

This arrangement proved difficult, however. The Barnwell School was huge: a thousand or so students, K-5. The small, close school family he knew at Ehrhardt Elementary was not so easily adopted in the larger setting. After two years, this part of his life was drawing to a close. He felt lost. He found some solace at, of all places, the nearby fitness center. Gladys would take him there, and he regimentally spent his self-imposed time limit on the New Step machine. One of the trainers was a young, powerfully built black man who had his own miraculous recovery story. He was kind and encouraging and took special interest in Gary.

It was nice to be only five minutes from school. As had always been, my principal gave me great liberty. If I needed to go home for any reason during my planning period or lunch break, I could go. Once when Gladys' husband was staying with Gary, I got a message: "When you get a chance, come home. But Gary's all right."

During lunch I rushed home to find termites swarming. Bernice had already filled my vacuum cleaner with them, but I had to find an exterminator immediately. Fortunately, our "bug man" who routinely sprayed the house was in the neighborhood. By late afternoon, the problem had been attacked before damage was done.

As in the past, our own brand of normalcy set in. I worked diligently in the yard, planting flowers and a kitchen garden. The lot that the house was on was small, and the in-ground pool took most of the back. Whoever put in the pool apparently had landscaping done, but all had been neglected over recent years. I did my best to bring the place some beauty and evidence of care. There were two huge Confederate rose bushes in the back. There was a rosebush and a few other plants, and there were even a few landscape lights (none of which worked), remnants of times when other owners had worked to beautify this sandy, porous spot of earth.

Somewhat paradoxically, we did these things, knowing that, within eight years or less, I would retire, and we would sell and move to the mountains. I also knew that pretty sells. Besides, who likes ugly? So I worked to make things attractive, and I enjoyed what I did.

I enjoyed the pool. I'm not a sun bather; I am a swimmer, so from April until October, I swam regularly, doing 10 to 15 laps. Then I was out of the water and on to the next thing on my list. However, I would never build a pool. They are expensive, require constant maintenance, and, like pets, can't be left unattended for long.

I was getting less sleep as Gary began to get up more at night. I was having to strip the bed more often. His "bathroom accidents" – times when he couldn't get to the bathroom quickly enough – seemed to become more frequent.

Where the Wisteria Grows

I had been sleeping in the adjacent room for some time – when I slept. In short, caregiving was becoming increasingly demanding. I had known for years there would come a time when I would not be able to care for him. Still, I did not see that in the immediate offing.

One day in early 2008 I saw my superintendent. She had been in the district since the 70s and had a formidable reputation as a political force. Yet when it came to her teachers, she was an equally formidable advocate. When my going got tough, she helped me to keep going, and I knew I was not the only one with whom she had been in the hard arenas. I appreciated her and knew I could depend on her. She knew how to get things done, whether others approved or not. On this day she said to me, "Why don't you go ahead and retire?"

I thought, "Gee, do I look that bad?" But I was startled. I had not given a thought to doing that. At least, not now. Sure, Carrie Michal would graduate in June, but I planned to work two or three more years.

"Carolyn, I don't have enough years," I said.

"When did you start?"

"In '79." Mentally she quickly tallied my years, picked up the phone and called the state retirement office, and within minutes turned to me and said, "You only lack three months. You can buy that out for..." I had an annuity I had started shortly after Gary got hurt. I took out less than $2,000 and said my goodbyes.

Where the Wisteria Grows

31
The Glade

I think there are only two ways to really see the world: walk or ride a horse. I have seen majesty while riding a horse, whether the black water swamps of the South Carolina Lowcountry, the red hills of the Upstate, the sand hills of the Pee Dee, or the Southern Appalachians. A seasoned hiker can walk many miles in flat land or piedmont land but not so many in the mountains. We have ridden our horses as much as 25 miles in the Cataloochee Valley of the Great Smoky Mountains National Park, crossing the pristine creeks in the valley, climbing to the Cataloochee Divide and looking down on Maggie Valley and across to peaks whose names we did not know, turning at Poll's Gap, where there is a spur from the Blue Ridge Parkway, on down an old railroad bed carved mostly by hand by the Civilian Conservation Corps in the early part of the 20th century, and making our way back to camp in the valley. The best of hikers would be challenged to walk so far, but for our steady Tennessee Walkers, this was a long but satisfying ride. We would be tired but content. We rode these trails with our good friend and true mountain man Benny Wines, whom we had met on the second of our trips to the valley. Benny was a true horseman, too. His family had been in Haywood County for generations. He knew the backbreaking work and toil of plowing rocky ground behind a horse, and the sweat and aches of staking tobacco. Most of the really good, steady reliable horses I ever owned were the ones Benny Wines found for me. He was a gentle honest man, and he would not put me on a horse he would not put his wife or his children on. When he called me and said, "I think I found ye a horse," I just hooked the trailer to the truck, for I was confident I would need it.

So it was that in July 2003 my close friend Pam Hutto, Carrie Michal, and a young friend from Ehrhardt made a trip to North Carolina to ride our horses. I had not come to buy; we had come to ride. God had always blessed us with wonderful caregivers to help with Gary and Mother: Charlotte, Mary, Betty Ann, who helped me for years, Susan Ford, and, after we moved to Barnwell, Gladys Ray and her husband. These were not just people who needed work; they were people who were willing to accept what I could pay, they loved Gary, and they did far more than just see that he was taken care of. They did laundry, washed dishes, made beds, and even cooked.

For me to have a few days away from the everyday, I had someone to depend on. Sure, I paid them, but the things they did were worth far more than I could pay. Beyond that, there were those in the community upon whom I called. If I needed to be out for a few hours, Bobbi Medlin, Betty Hiers, Carolyn Wilson, and others would come to the house and check on Gary and Carrie Michal, feed them, and just generally make sure all was safe.

So for a few days this hot July, we girls hauled our horses and gear to the mountains to ride. Because all of the horses did not have Coggins papers, we could not go in to Cataloochee. Benny said, "You can ride Beaverdam." I had no clue where that was, but I trusted him. We followed him through a lovely valley just outside of Canton, N.C., and, just as the valley began to lose its way to Beaverdam Mountain, we pulled the rig into the parking lot of Long Branch Missionary Baptist Church. "Jest ride up this road to the top 'a the mountain an' head down to Sandy Mush."

We saddled up and began riding. When we were in sight of the gap marking the top of the mountain, I noticed a rather nondescript sign whose paint had faded. "The Glade," the sign announced.

Something happened to me at that moment. An instant

Where the Wisteria Grows

powerful magnetism drew me, and I knew that, no matter how far my little mare carried me that day, I would return to The Glade.

We rode about six miles, going down into the pastoral valley known as Sandy Mush, in Buncombe County. Miles of clean farmland and dairy claim this valley, as well as the clean, sparkling waters of Little and Big Sandy Mush Creeks that bubble their way to somewhere – maybe the French Broad River. I don't know. I just know I felt I had entered an enchanted land, and I felt very much at home.

Later, as we made our way back, Benny's brother Bruce came creeping down Willow Creek Road "jest ta check on you'uns," he said. That was a good thing. Our flatland horses were tired, and Pam's gelding had almost given out. She was walking him when Bruce showed up. She sat on the tailgate of his truck and led her horse while the rest of us rode. When we finally reached the horse trailer, I said, "Bruce, if you have time before you go to work tonight, will you take me up to The Glade?"

"Why, shore." On that summer evening at dusk, I was taken to a world that seemed beyond this world, and certainly beyond any world I had ever dreamed of in this world. The beauty, peace, and perfection of this mountain entered my soul. In less than two years, we would own a home there. In three more years, we would live there in what I quickly came to call "Closer to Heaven."

Where the Wisteria Grows

32
Closer to Heaven

Bob Johnson was a retired Baptist minister, but, like most retired ministers who are still able to serve, he was always in the pulpit. His father was a minister, and so was his son. Ironically, his father had served the Ehrhardt Church as interim after Gary got hurt, and he served until he died suddenly of a heart attack. Later, Robert Johnson III was called as pastor at Ehrhardt.

Bob, Jr., was serving as interim at Bamberg in the early 2000s, after the Barnards moved away. He and his wife Patti were wonderful, gentle people with whom Gary and I immediately formed a bond. One Sunday night after church I said to them, "Come by the house and eat Sunday leftovers with us." They were the kind of home folks you could ask to do such a thing. I had always cooked Sunday dinner, in the tradition of my family, because we could not afford to eat out, because it was a long way to drive to a restaurant after Aunt Rachel's boarding house closed for a while after her death, and because Gary could no longer eat in public places because of his bathroom issues and anxiety.

During the course of conversation that evening, Bob casually mentioned having spent a weekend at The Glade. I interrupted him. "The Glade in Canton, N.C?"

"Yes," he replied, somewhat puzzled that I would know of the place. He told me a couple in a church in Hampton County, where he had served as interim, owned a home there, which they rented to relatives and friends.

So I said to Bob that Sunday night, "Give me their name and number."

That was in August of 2003. I called the owners, Teresa and Steve DeLoach, and rented the house for Thanksgiving. After that, we couldn't stay away. Every break I had from school we spent at The Glade. In '04 we spent the whole month of June on the mountain.

In March of '05, Teresa called. "Steve and I are praying about selling the mountain house, and we wanted to let you know first."

"When y'all get through praying, call me back," I said. Then I added, "And consider selling it as is."

"We hadn't thought of that. But we'll call you back."

She did. They gave us a price. "Gary and I will discuss it," I said. Gary said, "Buy it." He didn't even hesitate.

"We can't afford it!" I exclaimed.

"We can get the money," he said calmly.

"Yeah," I replied, "but can we pay it back?"

"Buy it," he repeated.

So we did. We had bought a lot on the mountain after we sold the house in Ehrhardt; we put it on the market. The realtor said, "Understand that it takes undeveloped property much longer to sell."

The property sold in six weeks. We made the down payment on Teresa's and Steve's house, took on a mortgage, and looked forward to the time when we would live in what Teresa had called "A Touch of Heaven" and which I rechristened "Closer to Heaven." Not a single obstacle came before us, and all of the transaction were done via fax and mail except the final signing, which Steve and Teresa did not even have to appear to do.

All of this was a few years before everything in our economic world crashed under the tsunamis of Fannie Mae, Freddie Mac, GM, and all of the other powerhouses deemed "too big to fail," and we taxpayers, through no vote of our own, became the fall guys. For most of us who are not investors, stock-market gamblers, or the other "important people," there was no clue.

Where the Wisteria Grows

Everyone I knew was like me, working, glad for our pay, taking care of our bills as best we could, and preferring to be left alone to live our daily days.

So it was in the spring of '08, with Carrie Michal's imminent graduation and my retirement, we put the house in Barnwell on the market. During June, I packed, sold a lot of "stuff" which I did not need and didn't want to move, and, setting June 26 as our moving date, worked toward that goal.

So many wonderful friends came to help the children and us load our household. I remarked to them at one point, "Thanks for your help. You must be really glad to see us go." They laughed and made a number of good comebacks, for they all knew my quick, often sardonic tongue.

During July and August I sold much of the furniture that had come with the mountain house. Steve and Teresa had furnished the house with sturdy, good, functional pieces that were perfect for the house and its setting. The house would sleep nine. They never lived in it. They had bought it for investment purposes – a good thing to do in the 90s if you could. We were the first people to actually live here.

During the quiet summer nights, with the windows and doors open (the house has no air conditioning; at 4,500 ft. elevation, it isn't very necessary), I felt such a peace and, even more, a sense of coming home. Like most Americans, we did not know of the catastrophe that was looming and would, within three months, crash upon us like a mountain mudslide.

Where the Wisteria Grows

33
Mountain Living

Shortly after we moved to the mountain, my friend Pam brought my horse up here. Eddie Maney had put up fencing on the lower part of the property. There was an outbuilding on the lower end that was easily adaptable for two stalls, so Eddie made those. Pam brought the black gelding I had bought earlier in the year, a six-year-old Tennessee Walker with a good reputation for steadiness and smooth gait. I also had a quarter horse I had bought for Carrie Michal, in hopes that she would get into barrel racing or cutting, which I had been told this horse would do.

Not. He was a nightmare in which I lost $2,000 over the next few years. I don't know if he had been abused in his younger years, but he was a problem from the get-go. Carrie Michal never trusted him, and neither did I nor anyone else who dealt with him.

This black gelding, however, was a dream. Not only was he beautiful and young, but also he was a perfect size for me. He had a long, curly black mane and tail. He enjoyed attention and being loved on, and I had no problem doing that.

Except I didn't have the time. Caregiving was increasingly demanding, and this horse really needed some ground work that I had neither the time nor expertise to provide. Between April and September of that year (2008), I broke a shoulder, an elbow, and a rib. The horse saw spooks, and I lost the confidence in the saddle I had once had. I was never an Annie Oakley, but for most of my life I felt secure and comfortable in the saddle or on the bare back of a horse. Anyway, my friend Mary Grace came and did some "ground work" with him and taught him some manners. I was still recovering from a broken elbow I had gotten when the horse did a sudden left turn from the gate. I was totally unprepared, so I hit the ground. Fortunately, Seth was there to take me to the ER. Gary was left by himself, which, at that time, was not the problem it would be three years later.

A few days later, Mary Grace called. "You wanna sell that horse?"

"Well, no, not particularly, but what do you have to offer?"

One of her riding students had fallen in love with "Mr. Sir." I sold him. I had learned over the years that I could sell most anything. I had discovered how transient and replaceable things are – even living things.

So I sold this beautiful animal, but I still had the old gelding of Carrie Michal's (Phoenix), that I had bought her for her 13th birthday. I also had the quarter horse gelding that had never been anything but a problem.

Eventually, I managed to get rid of the quarter horse and bring old Phoenix to the mountain. He was a joy to ride in this quiet, pure place.

Otherwise, we settled in here. I had big parties, mostly because that is what I like to do. I enjoy people, and I enjoy cooking. That is a proven combination for company. Cousins, neighbors, and friends came in and out. I found friends in Sandy Mush and Beaverdam, and soon gained access to fresh vegetables and even meat. Doug Howell and his boys shared deer, bear, grouse, turkey, and fish. I found people who grew garlic, other herbs, and, most importantly, shared themselves.

I don't think it is a hard thing to find people who care and share. Of course, I have never been known as quiet and shy. I have never been afraid to approach people and start a conversation. It is not so hard to do if you are willing to listen, pay attention, and remember you are with a significant person.

34
There All the Time?

You can drive along the same streets, roads, and highways every day for years, until everything along the way seems to become as familiar as your hands on the steering wheel. You hardly ever look to your right or left unless you have to stop at a light or stop sign.

For 23 years I traveled the lonely state highway 64 to school in Barnwell – 25 miles each way. Most of the traffic on any given day, morning or afternoon, was deer or tractors. The road is straight, for the most part, going through low-lying swamps, over black water streams, by thick pine woods and flat, open fields that lie fallow in the winter and pulse with corn, soybeans, and melons during growing season. In the late summer and into fall, combines weave their way down the highway and into the fields to harvest the corn and beans. Sometimes oats or wheat is planted after the harvest of the other crops. They soon become a brilliant, lush green, providing sharp contrast to the dull, dying leaves and weeds of November and December.

The children and I saw these changing yet changeless scenes, year after year, hardly ever really seeing them. After the time change in the fall, they would often be asleep as the VW Rabbit chugged through a dawn that was just coming on when we crossed the county line into Barnwell. Often I drove in the light of a setting moon behind me. Highway 64 goes almost due west, ending at the gates of the Savannah River Site at Snelling, just a few miles west of Barnwell. The road once was the main drag in a town called Ellenton that had been swallowed up by the government in the 50s when the SRS was developed. Now state highway 64 runs through the site itself.

The drive to school took 30 minutes. I was aware of old barns along the way, crumbling houses – tenant houses, as the locals called them, places where sharecroppers and farm laborers had once lived. There were a few places where a small grove of trees grew in the middle of a field. These trees were sometimes surrounded by a small iron fence, marking a family cemetery. The farmer who planted this field had to go around this small interruption in his path. One thing you don't do in the South is mess with a cemetery, especially a small family plot that holds the dust of those who left 150-200 years ago.

I was aware of every field, bridge, house (there were maybe a dozen or fewer houses between Ehrhardt and the Barnwell County line), and the people who lived there. I knew most of them. I knew where the deer usually crossed, and I was particularly vigilant there. I never hit a deer, but I knew plenty of people who had. Such a teté-a-teté between a deer and that little Rabbit could have wreaked quite a lot of damage on all of us.

However, no matter how often you travel the same way, every once in a while you see something you had never noticed. You didn't not notice it because it wasn't there; it had been there all along. How did you miss it? You've looked at that patch of woods for years and just now you see a small, dilapidated, weathered house with a collapsed porch and the remnants of a well just to the side. You get the feeling maybe some wood imps out there in the pines are being prankish.

This still happens when I drive the familiar roads here in the mountains, where I think I've seen everything along the way, and then one day I see something I've never noticed. It was there all the time.

Like life and the people in our lives. We go along, living our daily days, traveling well-worn paths, touching the people who are part of us, and suddenly there is something different, something we think may be new but it probably isn't. The place you think you

Where the Wisteria Grows

know completely has a dusty corner you hadn't seen before; the bed you moved so you could vacuum the dead men reveals a toy that had been missing so long you had forgotten about it. Where had it been? Trapped between the mattress and the sideboard or sitting on a slat all these years? That person you see every day, with whom you have worked for years, or with whom you have lived, that person who can absolutely never surprise you, because you know this person, inside and out. Except a moment comes and he or she does or says the totally unexpected. What that person says or does may not be as out of character as you think, for that behavior might possibly have been there all of the time.

I still have trouble believing Gary was at fault in that terrible accident. He was always a careful, calculating, defensive driver. He had always had a good handle on when it was time for aggression and when it was time to wait until you "see what the other person is going to do."

Yet it happened. Some events are serendipities, pleasant things that crop up while we are in the business of just doing what we are supposed to do, doing our jobs. Others crop up, and they are unpleasant, life-altering moments that, when we look back at them, we could say, "I do believe I could have lived better without that."

Where the Wisteria Grows

35
Knowing

Strange how there are some things you just know. You don't know them because they have already happened. You don't know them because you went down to Madame Rue's, the gypsy with the gold tattoo down at the corner. You don't know them because you had some epiphany one day at low tide. You don't know them the same way you know the baby is going to wet her diaper. (That's nature, the law of gravity, whatever.) You don't know because someone sent you a missive.

But you know. I knew Carrie Michal would finish Anderson University and follow what she believed in her heart God wanted her to do.

When the children were growing up, I felt the confidence that faith gives that the children would be God's first, ours next.

I knew there would come a time when, if Gary and I lived, I would be unable to take care of him. One thing I didn't consider was that one day I might not ride a horse again.

That's not written in stone yet.

For a while, I served a local church in town as pianist. However, the time came to move on. Didn't know where, but I knew it was time. Seth had moved in with us in the fall of '08, and that provided me with a freedom I would not have had otherwise.

He coached gymnastics in Asheville, and, since his classes were mostly in the afternoons, I could leave in the mornings and run errands or avail myself of other brief respites. On weekends, his presence and willingness allowed me to take a weekend off occasionally. He kept the grass cut and was here at night when I needed help with his dad.

Still, I knew he needed his own life, and although Gary was his dad, Gary was my husband. The relationship is not the same.

In May of '12, Seth accepted one of several offers he had received from various gyms. His excellent training with the Haydens when he was younger provided him with opportunities he may not have had otherwise. Plus, he is just a gifted teacher and coach, with a heart full of compassion and understanding.

He left. Within two days, Gary was in the hospital. From there, he went to Maggie Valley Rehabilitation for 100 days. He would never really be home again.

36
Accidents

They happen. They seem to happen to some people more often than others. We call such people "accident prone." I never considered myself one of those people. However, in recent years, my friends and my children would probably disagree. And the children have not shrunk from reminding me that my broken bones broke because of a horse, one way or another.

If I gave it much thought, I could picture myself as a Dick Van Dyke type, whose entrance into a room was tantamount to serious destruction.

Except Dick Van Dyke fell on purpose. And, he got famous and made serious money for his bruises.

I just – well, I just fell. Three times the horse spooked; once I was coming out of the barn and slid on the lawn-mower ramp, getting a deep puncture wound that my neighbor deemed needed stitches, which he would have never known except I ran out of medical tape and went to borrow some, so he overpowered me and took me to Urgent Care where I got seven stitches. Two summers ago I was going down to the barn to feed the horse before leaving for choir practice. It had rained that afternoon, and I had on white Keds with no traction. Down I went. Cousin Connie was spending a few days with me. I was able to walk back to the house. "I think I've sprained my ankle," I said calmly.

Calm, she wasn't. She immediately began to coerce me to Urgent Care. "No, just fix a foot tub. I have some Epsom Salts, so just get some warm water and let me soak." Naturally, she did not agree, but, after all, it was my foot.

During the night, pain changed my mind. After X-rays, the doctor said, "Well, you did a number on that right ankle."

So for the next two months, I needed a caregiver. As so many times before, Charlotte came. She stayed a month or so, and then dear Nancy drove all the way from Mississippi and stayed. They drove me to Maggie Valley to see Gary. They did laundry, cleaned, cooked, and tried hard to make me behave.

I had already applied for Medicaid. Gary's time at Maggie Valley was dictated by Medicare and his rehab progress. I knew I could not take care of him at home. The house was no longer equipped to accommodate him. Moreover, I still had a broken bone in the mending process.

Medicaid denied. I applied again. Medicaid denied. I spent down what little was left of his 403-B and closed out what I had, which was far less than what he had. I applied a third time, facing imminent discharge from Maggie Valley and having nowhere to go. Although we technically live in Buncombe County (the county line is in front of our house), our mailing address, phone, vehicle taxes, and even our voting precinct until last year have all been in Haywood County. So I applied at Haywood County Department of Social Services. By the time the third application went in, someone realized our property was in Buncombe County. Well, duh, my first application included our Buncombe County tax receipt. So now I had to apply in Asheville, having wasted three months putting applications in the wrong place.

Gary was discharged. I brought him home. I had no choice. Everyone knew this was a ready-made calamity. I could not afford the 24/7 help I needed, I was wearing a boot on my right foot, I could not get him in the shower, and Nancy had to go home. For the next several weeks, Haywood County EMS was up and down this mountain, sometimes just to get Gary off the floor where I'd dropped him, sometimes to take him to ER.

Meanwhile, in late September, Rita Kay's husband, who had

been diagnosed in June with mesothelioma, died. In desperation, I called Cheryl Vaughn, director at the Haywood House in Canton, a new memory care unit. She had taken Gary in for a few days after he had been admitted to the hospital, which had kept him for eight days because he had no safe place to go. Because I could not get help, I had to bring him home again. When my brother-in-law died, I called Cheryl. "We'll come and get him and take care of him until you get back."

I was gone for several days. Of course, when I returned, I picked up Gary and brought him home again. I could not pay for him to stay there. The calamity continued. He would fall, I'd call 911, and I suggested one night that the guys just stay parked in the driveway and spend the night. I'd cook biscuits and gravy for everybody.

Ha-ha.

Early on a Monday morning I called Cheryl again. "We'll come and get him." I'm sure there was no mistaking the desperation in my voice, and, truthfully, I did feel that I was coming apart. Poor Gary could see it, too, and he was as helpless as I.

Haywood House became his home, and, to a great extent, mine, too. The facility was only 20 minutes away, there were fewer than 25 residents, most of them women, and I found myself as busy there as I usually am anywhere else. Too often there were not enough hands to do what needed to be done, so I cleaned tables, mopped, helped serve, ran to keep someone who could not stand from trying to come out of a wheelchair, and took care of Gary, much as I had always done.

Except I had help if he fell. I had help so that he wouldn't fall. I often took him a meal, but, if I didn't, he was fed. I no longer had to stay up all night or most of the night. Many months later, I still didn't sleep all night, but I didn't have to change bed linens, get him in the shower at 4 a.m., or remind him it's 2 a.m. and not time to get up.

Where the Wisteria Grows

He lived there more than eight months with Medicaid pending.

Medicaid never happened. Because of the property in S.C. that had never sold, we could get no help. Our mortgage there had been sold out two years earlier to Bank of America. (No one asked us if we wanted to belong to them.) I knew I had to do the extreme to get this property out of our names: foreclose. We owed around $73,000 and had been able to make the monthly payments because of good tenants.

So one day I took a copy of the title to the property (which I had requested from the Clerk of Court in Barnwell County) to the nearest Bank of America branch, went into the mortgage officer's office, laid the copy down and said, "Foreclose, immediately. Don't talk to me about loan assistance; that will not help us."

She was a young, attractive, smart woman, and she was clearly stunned. Her dark eyes regarded me intently. "Sit down," she said. I did. I began a concise summary of our situation. I say concise, but with the turmoil of our circumstance, conciseness was a challenge to which I never could have risen without my educational background. In undergraduate work, I had languished under Dr. William O'Cain's course in Modern American Grammar. He was a native of Orangeburg, S.C., and had the beautiful and soft speech cadence of educated, Lowcountry natives whose generations included the old aristocratic planter class of antebellum days. He taught me (at the expense of much red ink) these things about writing: brevity, clarity, and precision.

Not saying I mastered these. But I learned: never use six words if three will do. For example: why say "Due to the fact that," when "because" will do the job?

So I explained to this young woman why nothing would help except foreclosure or "deed-in-lieu," a term I would quickly learn yet never, to this day, quite understand how it differs from foreclosure.

It took eight months for this process to complete. I won't even take up the space to explain all of the turn-arounds, lost communications, crossed and criss-crossed paths, but, while the lender was trying to figure this out from Brussels, Shangpo, the Balkans, or wherever, we were sold out again. I was served notice that Gary would be discharged from Haywood House May 31 for nonpayment (around $21,000) and, once again, we had nowhere to go. I had paid what I could every month for Gary's care, but who can touch $6,000-8,000 a month?

On May 30, I was scheduled for a hearing, via conference call, with the corporate managers of Haywood House. I had heard nothing from the deed-in-lieu, although I called, wrote, and emailed regularly. Without it, there was no need to go re-apply at DSS. Without a three-day stay in the hospital, there was no way to relocate to another facility. Gary was not sick, so there was no reason to take him to the hospital. It occurred to me how ironic and frustrating the situation was. He was too healthy! I had made up my mind to bring him home, as calamitous as everyone knew that would be. The administrators at Haywood House were trying hard to find us a place to go, but that didn't matter. I simply had no resources to pay for his care. I surrendered a small life insurance policy I owned. There was nothing to tell the corporate reps but, "We'll go home." I knew that, even if we stayed there and finally got Medicaid, it would not be retroactive; I would still carry the debt that had piled on for months.

We often (sometimes blithely and tritely) say, "God moves in mysterious ways." But he does, and, in my experience, he moves at the 11th or even the 13th hour. This is a very frustrating truth. Of course, I can't see how he may have been constructing this road while I was stressed out, anxiety-ridden, and at my wit's end. I guess I've still got a lot to learn about calm trust.

I went in to the Haywood House to see Gary on May 23. I knew immediately something was wrong. He was confused, weak, slow to respond – all the symptoms I had come to recognize as a urinary tract infection.

Where the Wisteria Grows

He was whisked to the hospital, tested and tried, and, sure enough, had the infection that necessitated intravenous antibiotic.

Three days later, he was discharged. Because of the holiday (Memorial Day), we had to return to Haywood House. I had no idea where we would go from there, but now the door had been opened for Medicare to cover placement, at least for a while.

Then another answer came, ringing in about the same time as the conference call. A friend whom we had not seen in a while came by the facility to see us. We sat outside in "Nancy's Garden," just chatting. As she overheard the conversation and listened to the situation, she finally said, "I work for the admissions person at Autumn Care. Want me to call her?" Autumn Care is a fine skilled-care facility about 30 minutes from the house. It had been my first choice for placement, for it had a good reputation both as skilled and rehab unit, and it was in the county.

"How fast can you dial that number?"

In less than an hour, an evaluation was set up for the next morning.

By June 1, we were moved in to Autumn Care. This was now the third facility Gary had been in in just over a year. It was hard, but God had opened doors. I see such relocation somewhat analogous to moving children from one foster home to another.

Except we are not children. We are adults who have lived together, worked together and intimately and passionately been so much a part of each other that any separation, no matter how well you understand its necessity, invokes a real process of grief, loss, and indescribable adjustments.

Here but gone.

Where the Wisteria Grows

37
Autumn Care

At the end of July Gary was discharged from therapy services at the facility. That meant Medicare would no longer pay. After long months of dogged, persistent pursuit, I had finally received the deed-in-lieu for the Barnwell property. I immediately went to DSS to re-apply for Medicaid.

By August we had been approved. There was just one not-so-small-at-all problem: because my income was $211 over the allowed amount, our liability at Autumn Care would be more than $1,300 a month. That was more than our house payment. It came to me that (a) he could have a home and I wouldn't, or (b) he could come home and both of us have a home.

In the process of applying for assistance, I had used the money from our 403-Bs and my insurance policy to pay on the large debt we had accrued at the Haywood House. The 19 cents we had in a savings account I had never gotten around to closing wasn't going to do much toward that monthly liability.

So, on September 17, we came home again. I was able to get a $500 voucher from a regional respite care agency. That was good for a year. I spent close to half of that on the 21st to go to Anderson for Carrie Michal's 24th birthday. She was singing in a community choir that holds a concert every year for the Cancer Society. I had bought a ticket weeks earlier. I left that Saturday around 11:30 in the morning and returned at midnight.

The next day we spent seven hours in the ER. Another urinary tract infection. The next Sunday I called EMS. Gary was wheezing like a severe asthmatic. I could hear him all over the house.

This time he was admitted and kept for four days while all kinds of tests were made. He was given breathing treatments every two hours for the first two days and then every four to six hours. This was all very hard, for, as always, he didn't feel bad, and, truthfully, neither of us realized how sick he was. As I explained to him, "Hospitals don't keep you these days unless you are sick."

Because more than two months had passed since he had been covered by Medicare, he was able to be discharged back to Autumn Care. I knew when he was discharged from rehab services we would have to come home again. I also knew what that meant – for both of us.

In so many ways, where he is now is the best place for us. There are activities all during the week; he is getting some therapy; he is cared for by people who truly love him, for he is easy to love; he can interact with others, residents and staff who know him by name, speak to him, and show friendliness.

Nothing in all of this is easy for me: the loneliness and emptiness that only he can fill, the feeling that shoots through me that our days and nights are not supposed to be this way, that the whole picture has too many shadows. We should be enjoying the theater, music, books, and grandchildren together. We should be keeping each other warm on these cold winter nights on the mountain, taking walks in the snow, holding each other in the security only enduring love provides.

But the way I think things should be is not the way they are. Except the immortality of the love itself.

Where the Wisteria Grows

38
Celebrities

Dolly Parton
Diane Sawyer
Robin Roberts
Carol Burnett
Loretta Lynn

These are famous people I would like to meet. Four of them are bona fide Southerners, and Carol Burnett was actually born in Texas, so that counts. Here are other reasons: they have made their own way, with hard work, determination, real talent, and plain grit. None of them came from families of power and privilege. In fact, the opposite is more true. Beyond that, they seem to naturally exude warmth, honesty, and a sense of compassion. If they stepped on anyone to get where they are, I have never heard of or read it, and such behavior certainly would not fit the image they portray. I, for one, believe in their integrity, even with Dolly's fake hair and the trappings that she freely and laughingly jokes about, knowing they are part of who she is, but they are not her.

The main thing I would like to do is have them come and sit in my kitchen, eat collards, cornbread, and smoked venison, or whatever they would like, and then gather around the piano or sit outside and sing along with me and my guitar. And talk, of course.

No, there are no men on my celebrity list. I don't know why. Maybe Garrison Keillor could be one; he can sing, and he can certainly talk, although he's from Minnesota and was probably a Lutheran. He may still be a Lutheran.

Truth is, I've seen more celebrities in the past year than could ever be on TV or the cover of some magazine. They are not famous people. I don't know if any of them are rich, but I doubt it, for I've seen them in nursing homes. Some live there. Many of them don't know they live there, for age and cruel diseases have robbed them of the present.

The other celebrities are those who come often, sometimes daily, to see that once-beautiful woman who will always be beautiful to them yet who may not recognize them. These celebrities walk in with love written all over them, and they sit with mother, father, grandmother, aunt, sister, brother, and there is so much tenderness, so much gentleness, and so much patience. These celebrities take time to push the wheelchair around, or take mama for a ride. Many of them take home the soiled laundry, bringing it back fresh and clean. They pick up the spoon to bring food to auntie's mouth, or, if she can feed herself, they lovingly encourage her to "eat, so you won't get sick."

Often there is much sickness, for age is not always kind. Many of the celebrities who live here have invested their lives in others: family, friends, community. The recipients of their love and devotion now come to see the one who, for many reasons, is still a famous person in the sense that he or she not only gave of themselves to enrich others, but also bestowed a heritage time cannot steal nor a thief purloin. There are those who have been "dumped on the doorstep," where the door closed and no one from the outside came back to open it. But I've seen only one or two.

Mostly, that is not what I have seen. The vast majority of people I have come to know, appreciate, and respect, are the celebrities I see every day in a place where the camera never goes.

Where the Wisteria Grows

39
Sun and Shadows

Spring is green and gold, which is odd, since much of autumn is gold. "Nature's first green is gold...but nothing gold can stay" (Robert Frost). Spring bows to summer, where an August noon is so still you can hear the sound of the silence, and, in the South, feel the shimmering heat bathing your skin from every direction. You can retreat to your air-conditioned comfort, but when you walk out the door of that cool sanctuary, southern summers show no mercy.

Here on the mountain, summer begins to retreat in late August. The underbelly of locust tree leaves begins to show a dull rust color, and I know soon there will be the very yellow days of September, when I will need extra cover on the bed at night and less cover on me during the day. The native wildflowers will come forth with a final shout and show themselves shamelessly, like a gilded prostitute. The wind will lie so still I can hear the yellow invisibly painting the world in a glory untouchable by the artist's hand. God has his own palette and color scheme.

These yellow days give way steadily to approaching winter. Here on the mountain, leaves begin to fall in early September. Sunlight becomes muted, and its light weaves in and out of the shadows of the colored leaves, like an elusive will-o'-the-wisp. Sometimes light snow falls in late October. Cold fronts from the North begin to blow across the mountain, often with a vengeance. Some winters are harsh and bitter; others – not so much.

Our lives are so much like the seasons. We move from one stage to the next, darting in and out of shadows, passing through painful dark days into the brightness joy brings. There are times when seasons and lives end too soon, like days in April that remain cold and gray, as if winter has taken an extended stay.

We really don't know much about life. We live it until we die; we work, have families, celebrate the holidays, look forward to time off and times that are less stressful and demanding, learn many of life's lessons, but we have no way of knowing what lies beyond the hills or in the dark, scary places like tunnels and blind curves. We often think we are the engineers, fully in control of the throttle, our eyes on the tracks ahead.

Then we derail, and the whole train and its cargo are damaged at best, gone forever, at worst. We couldn't eliminate all of the variables. I think our inability to do that is God's reminder to us that He holds tomorrow.

So, I didn't know exactly what would happen. Gary was cared for, but I had no guarantee the resources would remain. Assistance with the exorbitant costs of health care becomes increasingly tenuous in our imploding society.

These things I do know: Life is a garden into which we are born. We are placed there for a purpose: to reach out and touch others with kindness, gentleness, forgiveness, compassion, encouragement, and love. We have a responsibility to plant, to cultivate, and to keep weeds, harmful bugs and other critters, and disease out. Spring folds into summer, summer into autumn, autumn into winter. Rain falls, sun warms, winds blow, and nature's cycle spins from dormancy to bloom to death, and we don't have control of those forces. We do choose what we plant and how we manage and feed our garden.

Just outside of Ehrhardt there is a towering live oak tree a few feet from the road. Spanish moss hangs like long tresses from the long, twisting branches. At the bottom of the tree the thick, knobby root of a wisteria vine found its home many years ago. Now the old oak is wrapped by the vine that has grown around every limb of its body. Every spring the tree becomes dressed in finery worthy of a Mardi Gras queen, wearing her own gold and thousands of white and violet wisteria blooms dangling like rare jewels, emitting their sweet, subtle perfume – looking and smelling so fine with her hair of Spanish moss that briefly loses its own drabness.

Interestingly, that tree has not been strangled by its bossy, nosy neighbor. Indeed, it has risen above it, sometimes just barely, but growing tall and strong, losing a few limbs and leaves here and there, but alive – and well.

An old spiritual says, "Soon ah will be done wid de troubles of de world." Sometimes that time comes sooner than we thought. In the meantime, we live with those troubles, we give in to those troubles, or we take the lessons they can teach us and make them strong plants to give us loveliness and sweet perfume.

Where the Wisteria Grows

Epilogue

"Over" is a word that means what it says, yet doesn't. Much of my family's life was "over" the day a tractor trailer rammed into Gary on a wet Virginia highway in 1990. However, much was not "over," for we forged our way into a different life, adopting skills to enable us to not only survive but also to produce, serve, grow, manage.

On September 28, 2014, Gary died, after nine days of sepsis and a failing heart. There was no pain, no regret, and no fear – for him, for me, for the children. During those days of waiting, I was reminded again and again of how tenacious life is, how it stubbornly defies the steadily encroaching tentacles of death, seeming to shake its weakening fist saying, "Not yet! Not yet!"

Immortality rests with none of us. The best we can hope to do is live each moment of each day with gratitude, a spirit of forgiveness, a sense of wonder, and a keen awareness of and sensitivity to faith in a God whose grace is greater than our failures, and whose love reaches beyond our fears, needs, griefs, and disappointments.

Paradoxically, to live such a life does create a kind of immortality, for in such living we build legacy and a sense of goodness that lives after us. The good is not always "interred with our bones," as Antony says of Caesar.

The strength, love, integrity, and wisdom of their father now live in our children and in the minds and hearts of the many lives he touched. Love is, indeed, "an ever-fixéd mark/that looks on tempests and is never shaken..."

For the Watsons— forever
friends — with love, appreciation,
and great gratitude for a
lifetime of support, en-
couragement, and loyalty—
and with thanks to God for
your lives of giving to others,
of faith, and commitment to
Our God whose grace is
greater than our failures.
Renee Mullins

1/15

18305655R30080

Made in the USA
San Bernardino, CA
09 January 2015